The Legendary

APPALOOSA

A TRIBUTE IN WORDS AND PHOTOS

CHERYL DUDLEY

The Lyons Press
Guilford, Connecticut

An imprint of The Globe Pequot Press

To my husband, Don,
and my sons Jason, Jeremy, Joel, and Jesse

To buy books in quantity for corporate use
or incentives, call **(800) 962–0973**
or e-mail **premiums@GlobePequot.com.**

The Lyons Press is an imprint of The Globe Pequot Press.

10 9 8 7 6 5 4 3 2 1

Printed in China

Designed by Sheryl P. Kober

ISBN: 978-1-59921-048-3

Library of Congress Cataloging-in-Publication Data is available on file.

Table of Contents

Foreword

The Legendary Appaloosa is a blend of interesting text and authentic photographs of the Appaloosa horse. Important events in Appaloosa history are covered, along with a wide range of the significant aspects of the breed. This book analyzes what the Appaloosa is and does and where it is in today's world.

Since the coffee table became widely popular, there is a need for "coffee table" books to entertain both family and guests. However, given the textual content combined with the quality of the photographs in *The Legendary Appaloosa*, this book is well qualified for both the coffee table and the family bookshelf.

—GEORGE HATLEY

George Hatley's involvement with the Appaloosa Horse Club ranges over 40 years. He served as executive secretary for 31 years and was the first editor of the *Appaloosa News*. He published the first Appaloosa stud book and worked to develop the Chief Joseph Trail Ride. He was also manager of the first National Appaloosa Sale and the first National Appaloosa Show in Lewiston, Idaho. George and his wife Iola bred several well-known horses, including Apache Double, a successful racing competitor. They both continue to serve on the Appaloosa Museum board and remain involved with horse activities on the Palouse, including sponsoring the Apalousey Trail Ride each year on their property near Deary, Idaho.

Acknowledgments

A special thanks to "Mr. Appaloosa" George Hatley for his guidance, wisdom, and insight into writing this book. Truly a historic man in the Appaloosa world, his kind heart and gentle spirit made working with him on this project an absolute joy.

This book would not be possible without the contribution of countless Appaloosa owners who love the horse and are dedicated to the breed. The enthusiasm to take and contribute photographs of their horses was amazing, and I am eternally grateful for each contributor. I hope that the variety of perspectives offered to readers through the eyes of these different photographers will help portray the versatility, color, conformation, personality, and talent of the Appaloosa. I want to especially thank my son Jason Abbott for photos and everything else I asked him to do, including PhotoShop work and advice, along with Jessica Wright, Kevin Pullen, Lisa Estridge, Jan Bard, Kim Utke, Ursula Lise, Monika Hannawacker, Jeri Rainer, Sue Schembri, Victoria Ennis, Mary Sue Kunz, Liz Kinkaid, Kim Welch, Kristin Reiter, and Jillian Paige Dunkleberger for sharing their photos. There is a short bio of each photographer in the back of the book. I'd also like to thank Larry Williams and Gene Wilson & Associates.

I'm also grateful to my husband, Don Dudley, for his support, patience, and encouragement; my sisters, Diana Thornton and Jackie Bolden, for their inspiration and input; Diane Rice, for helping me get all the facts right; Jennie Wandler, for reading the manuscript and giving me feedback; and to Laura Vander Ploeg, for helping with photos.

I grew up galloping bareback on a snowflake Appaloosa across the Palouse hills of North Idaho. A gift from my dad when I was 10 years old, this horse fulfilled some of my greatest needs as a small girl and later as a confused teen. My mare Snowflake provided the companionship and quiet understanding I longed for during those impressionable years. She always responded to my ramblings with a gentle eye and attentive ear, and I believed she understood me when no one else did.

Snowflake and I explored the deep tamarack forests, snowcapped mountaintops, rolling hills, and lush ponds of the Palouse. To this day I swear I know every rich secret this beautiful landscape possesses. I will always have an intense feeling of oneness with Snowflake because of our experiences. Not only did I root out the beauty of nature on our adventures, I dug down to my own spirit and discovered how I fit into a world that seemed so bewildering back then. Snowflake was with me through it all.

Snowflake is still as present in my heart as she was powerful in my young life. She lived to be nearly 32 years old, bought by an elderly farmer as a broodmare after I married and moved away from home. Even though I've had horses since then and own several now, there's something about my first horse connection that I'll never forget. I know I am not alone.

This book is for Snowflake and for all who understand what I mean when I say there is something distinctive about an Appaloosa horse. I've experienced it firsthand. It's also for my dad, who passed away years ago, and was wise enough to work many overtime hours to buy his little girl a horse when she needed something in life he didn't really understand.

My goal in writing this book is to share with you not just the amazing beauty and story of the Appaloosa, but the majestic place where it originated and its versatile roles in the lives of people worldwide. I hope you discover, like I did, that the Appaloosa horse truly is legendary.

Christine Nelson riding Ristow at an open breed show, Princeton, Idaho. Photo by Kevin Pullen.

AN AMERICAN PRESENCE

The Legend

Beauty, endurance, intelligence, speed, versatility, and athleticism—the Appaloosa has it all. The Appaloosa horse is an icon of the early West and the current-day choice for those seeking a full package of equine abilities, accented by a palette of colors and coat patterns unique to the breed.

Just as important as brilliant colors and talents is the Appaloosa's ability to connect with humans and create deep and lasting bonds that can change lives and heal hearts. Known for their calm, unshakable demeanor and a sensibility that goes beyond other breeds, Appaloosas partner with people for life's adventures both as best friends and unforgettable companions.

Many stories have been told of the Appaloosa horse and its connection to the Nez Perce Indians of the American Northwest. While we often hear of selective breeding programs, the incredible stamina and hardiness of this rugged mountain horse, and its importance in hunting and war, we seldom hear about what the horse meant to the women and children of the tribes.

Kaden Abbott at Gramps Appaloosas, owned by Roy Scoles, Princeton, Idaho. Photo by Jason Abbott.

The relationship-seeking heart of women is universal. Trying to imagine what it was like to rely on a horse for mobility is like trying to imagine the need to hunt for food each

NARHA-certified instructor Sharlene Adams with her Appaloosa, Oliver. Dixie River Ranch, Caldwell, Idaho. Photo by Jason Abbott.

day. Women today enjoy their horses in a whole different way than the Native American women must have. But I imagine the Native American women's relationships with their horses as even more powerful than ours, because any time reliance exists between two lives, a strong bond occurs.

Out of these women's untold stories of horse-human relationships blossom imaginary tales of first encounters that evolved into meaningful and lasting relationships.

Spirits Mingled

The meager girl, not much bigger than the native pups that frolicked along the Wallowas, approached the newly captured horse, her tiny palm open and extended as if to offer more than a caress upon his velvety muzzle. Inching forward cautiously in soft deerskin moccasins, trembling with the anticipation of that first touch, her wide eyes told the whole story of why she entered the pen of the wild horse: fascination, hope, longing. Through her veins pulsed the tender desire to be worthy of the stallion's presence and to capture his noble spirit and make it hers. ◆ The charcoal-black stallion with a splash of white across his hips and loins arched his neck and snorted at the small replica of his captors, tossed his head and mane to the wind, and stomped the ground as a warning to the girl to keep her distance. Suddenly frightened, the small girl sat down in the trampled grass, buried her head between her arms, and quietly sobbed. ◆ Yards away in the village, a mother searched frantically for her missing daughter. Knowing the dangers of the rugged mountains, every terrifying scenario of what could happen raced through her mind as she ran, calling out her child's name. Before long the whole village searched, called, cried out for the girl. By the time they reached the pen of the wild horse where the girl sat, they stood breathless, frantic, and in silent wonder, not knowing what to do. ◆ The majestic stallion, head down, eyes now soft, tenderly nuzzled the girl's braided hair and billowed his warm breath against her cheek. While the tribal elders stiffened and clenched their hands, the girl looked up into the gentle stallion's eyes, raised her hands to his face, and finally stroked his black muzzle. ◆ "You will be my best friend forever," she whispered prophetically. ◆ The men of the village went on to breed many of their mares to the stallion, populating the land with spotted foals valuable for hunting, packing, and racing. These spotted horses became known for their strength and sure-footedness in the rugged mountains and for their desire to partner with people. Selectively bred for these characteristics, the spotted stallion's progeny became prized possessions among the tribes. ◆ But they could never match the legendary story the sire carried with his name, of the day he comforted the lost, brokenhearted girl. He became Nimiipuu Sikem, the sire of the magnificent Native American *spotted horse. But to the little girl, his spirit coexisted with hers in an eternal place that transcended time and space.* ◆ *The girl grew up riding the stallion. When she walked to the edge of the field and called his name, his eye would fix on her and he'd come running, tail high, nickering her name back as if he'd been anticipating their reunion. She often sat in the fields and watched him graze, just to feel his presence. He journeyed with her through her childhood, and their hearts mingled as one into her womanhood.*

These co-mingled spirits sparked an ember that still glows in the hearts of Appaloosa lovers worldwide. The Appaloosa's desire to please, understand, and connect with their human partners outstrips all our awkward desires to control them. Their magnificent color may capture our eye, but their spirit surely captures our hearts.

Deviney Wynecoop, Wellpinit, Washington. Photo by Jeri Rainer.

The Legacy Begins

At the dawn of civilization, spotted horses loped over the horizon, stamping an impression on human history. Long before early people entertained the idea of domestication, they admired the spotted horses for their unusual color and coat patterns. Early civilizations decorated their cavern walls with artistic drawings of plump, multi-colored mares covered with spots—paintings that have survived eons of time and tell us an ancient story of intrigue.

Mares at Sheldak Ranch, Sheldon, North Dakota. Photo by owner Kim Utke.

This age-old story is the precursor of a historic partnership between the human race and the spotted horse that facilitated world-changing events down through history. Soon people tamed the horse and called it friend—a harmonious existence that throughout the centuries evolved from a partnership in battle and survival to a partnership in the show ring, on the racetrack, on the working ranch, and on the trail.

Transported to the Americas by Spanish conquistadors, the American spotted horse is said to have descended from exotic royal bloodlines dating back to early European nobility. The history of the spotted horse eventually became embedded in the roots of American Northwest history, linked with the Native tribes who first populated the beautiful, mysterious, and rugged country of Washington, Idaho, Montana, and Oregon.

Native Americans prized horses for strength, endurance, and sure-footedness and purposely bred them for these characteristics. The absence of these characteristics would have rendered a horse worthless in such country. There is no doubt that the attributes of the spotted horse proved valuable for hunting buffalo on the plains of Montana and for survival among the mountains of the American Northwest. In

CL Hart to Hart, "Lawyer," a Joker B. descendent. Owned by Vivian Knowles, Last Hurrah Ranch, Tensed, Idaho. Photo by Kevin Pullen.

wartime, the spotted horse offered the agility and athleticism necessary for victory—with a unique beauty unlike any other American horse.

The Nez Perce called their horse "Nimiipuu Sikem," translated as "a new breed." Every spotted horse that grazed along the Palouse River and roamed the rolling hills of the region came to be called "A Palouse Horse" by the white man, which in time slurred to "Apalousey" and later evolved to its current name, Appaloosa.

Contemporary Appaloosas

Sixty years after the territorial war between the United States Cavalry and the Northwest's non-treaty Indian bands that dispersed the spotted Indian horses, efforts ensued to re-establish the near-extinct Appaloosa breed in 1938. The genesis of this effort began with the formation of the Appaloosa Horse Club (ApHC) by Oregon Appaloosa-lover Claude Thompson. Along with six charter members, Claude began to breed back into existence the spotted equine masterpiece. Under the guidance and leadership of George Hatley, the ApHC grew quickly over the next 30 years,

Mare and foal at Sheldak Ranch, Sheldon, North Dakota. Photo by owner Kim Utke.

placing Appaloosa horses among the top American breeds. In 1975 the Appaloosa horse, so tied to the Palouse area through the history of the local Indian tribes and later the Appaloosa Horse Club, was proudly named the Idaho State Horse.

While many breeders crossed their Appaloosas with other breeds during these years, several chose to stick with Appaloosa-to-Appaloosa breeding. These separate breeding programs continue today.

In 1996 New Mexico Appaloosa breeder Bob Browning gave the Nez Perce Indian tribe an excellent band of Appaloosa mares. Soon four Akhal-Teke stallions, athletic horses similar to Thoroughbreds in conformation, were acquired from Germany. An ancient Asian breed similar to the original Spanish horses that arrived in the U.S., these horses excel in endurance, racing, jumping, and dressage. By mating the

Marge Bibeau riding A&B Skips, owned by Marge and Julie Bibeau. Heritage Class, 2006 Appaloosa National Show. Photo by Jennie Wandler.

Akhal-Teke stallions to the Appaloosa mares, the Nez Perce tribe attempted to re-create their "Nez Perce Horse," which is similar in conformation to the horses they had bred prior to the Nez Perce war of 1877.

In 1997 the first Akhal-Teke/Appaloosa horses were foaled. The Nez Perce established a registry for keeping pedigree records of their horses and formed the Nez Perce Appaloosa Horse Club, which teaches horsemanship to youths and sponsors trail rides, games, and riding groups that participate in parades and tribal functions. Through these efforts, the Nez Perce tribe is attempting to re-establish its past reputation for good horse breeding and horsemanship.

The remarkable Appaloosa horse has found its way into the lives of horse lovers worldwide, representing all facets, from trail riding, hippotherapy, and pasture

Kaden Abbott, Gramps Appaloosas, owned by Roy Scoles, Princeton, Idaho. Photo by Jason Abbott.

pets to showing, endurance riding, and racing. While many breeders have determined to maintain the foundation bloodlines of the Appaloosa as closely as possible, other breeders have successfully crossed the Appaloosa with Quarter Horses, Arabians, Thoroughbreds, and others, resulting in amazing show-winning bloodlines and sculpted racing conformations.

Through the efforts of the Appaloosa Horse Club and Appaloosa breeders worldwide, the Appaloosa horse gains more popularity each year. The Appaloosa Horse Club has fulfilled its mission to salvage a horse worthy of its heritage as a beautiful, athletic, and intelligent companion.

Showcasing the Appaloosa's rich and intriguing history and its many roles in contemporary life, this look at the Appaloosa horse covers the whole spectrum, from its ancient beginnings to its athletic ability, color and conformation, and companionship.

Indeed, no other breed of horse shares such a tragic, yet glorious, history or can claim such beauty and versatility as the majestic icon of the Palouse—the Appaloosa.

Leading sire Imaginate, at Sheldak Ranch, Sheldon, North Dakota. Photo by owner Kim Utke.

The dews drop slowly and dreams gather: unknown spears suddenly hurdle before my dream—awakened eyes . . . and then the clash.

—W. B. YEATS

Ancient History

From a distance, the herd of horses flashed in the afternoon light, a brilliant array of magnificent colors, sure-footed, stocky, and athletic in their movements. New spring foals—most would eventually look like their sire: deep red with a white spotted hip blanket—stretched their small necks to reach the new grass. It was easy for the men to become mesmerized by the beauty of the animals and forget their mission: to bring meat home to their clan. ♦ *The horse embodied something different from the other prey animals the men hunted, something that the men didn't understand but were drawn to. Sometimes they felt as if the horse could read their minds. There was even a story of one man who had walked up to a horse and touched it—a touch that he'd said sent warmth through his whole being and made him give up hunting the horse all together.* ♦ *Spears in hand, the men crept closer to the herd,*

stopping often to scope out the one horse that looked easy prey. There she was—a large, plump mare with a foal at her side in easy range. The foal would find a surrogate mother, they hoped, and the mare would provide good sustenance for the women and children at home. ♦ *Of the three men, it was the youngest who was chosen to make the kill. This was his first hunt, and the two older men had worked with him to make his spears straight*

Photo by owner Monika Hannawacker, Germany.

and sure. With the mare's stance, the arrow would make a quick kill. She wouldn't suffer. ◆ *The young man slowly stood and readied himself to launch the spear, but just then a ray of sun broke from behind the clouds and shone on the herd, lighting the white in their coats to a soft glow. The mare raised her head and looked at the young man just then. He was close enough to see the white in her eyes and the smooth slope of her forehead. He noticed the white tips of her ears, flaring nostrils, the curve of her neck and hip, and the strong white legs that had carried the foal until a few days ago. He noticed her color—mostly white with dark spots—and took note of her uniqueness. He wondered what it would be like to tame her, as they had tamed other animals, and he found himself longing to walk up and touch her.* ◆ *The two elder hunters nudged the young man to make his kill. Now was the time, since in a second the herd would be running. The young man pushed his desires down to a place where, for now, he could forget about them, but secretly vowed to bring them back and dwell on them later. Not wanting to disappoint the elders, for now he had to push aside his feelings and focus on the hunt.* ◆ *As the hunter launched the spear, for one last time the mare reached down and brushed her face against the softness of her newborn foal.*

Mare and foal at Sheldak Ranch, Sheldon, North Dakota. Photo by owner Kim Utke.

The Hunter, owned and photographed by Sue Schembri of Char-O-Lot Ranch, Florida.

Spotted horses are known to date back to the Cro-Magnons—mighty western European hunters who tracked grazing animals across the newly melted pasturelands of the ice age. As the ice melted and retreated, the resulting flowing streams cut deep passageways through the plateaus, carving great cliffs, ledges, and caverns that stretched for miles and offered shelter for the early people. Paintings in these shallow caves and caverns in central France, dated around 18000 B.C., depict a profusion of

animals, including red, brown, and tan spotted horses. These paintings were part of the rituals practiced by the Cro-Magnons to ensure ample crops of foals and calves each year. Archeological diggings in the caves revealed that before they were domesticated, wild horses were part of the Cro-Magnon's diet. Little did people know then, the spotted horse would one day become highly important to their survival in an aggressively growing world—far beyond a food source.

Around 5000 B.C., after the ice sheet melted and revealed ample pasture and steppe country, hunters learned to trap herds of grass eaters within the natural gorge barriers formed by the melting ice and to build fences. This allowed hunters to raise their own meat supplies and to tame some of the herd animals as well. The first known domestic herd animals were the reindeer and the wild ass.

Mesopotamians domesticated cattle, sheep, and goats, and also developed the wheel. Soon, oxen and horses were taught to pull carts. As nomadic tribes moved to new locations daily, it's reasonable to assume that many of them became competent horseback riders who learned to round up and move the camp's herds. These horsepeople might be considered analogous to American West ranchers.

Along the eastern edge of the Asiatic steppes, more primitive tribes established themselves in fertile areas frequented by herds of grazing animals. Preferring to stay put, these tribes seemed content to live a slow-paced life, and had not yet learned the mobility that domesticated horses could offer. Before long, however, cartloads of nomadic families led by domesticated horses appeared on the western horizon, introducing to the Asian tribes this new mobility. Because of the geology of the landscape, these primitive tribes found that riding horses suited them well as opposed to riding in horse-drawn carts. The foothills tribespeople were smaller and lighter than the westerners, making them better horseback-riding candidates.

As horse-drawn war chariots began to invade Mesopotamia from the Asiatic steppe land, other groups of warriors entered Egypt, frightening the native people, who had never seen such strange animals. Eventually, though, the Egyptians assimilated the horse and chariot into their own culture. Egyptian pictures and Mycenae art from around 1400 B.C. show spotted horses. The spotted horse later appeared in Austria and northern Italy, and by 500 B.C. they appeared regularly in Chinese art, on intricate vases and wall hangings.

The horse culture spread quickly to the north and east and eventually reached Mongolia, allowing free-traveling nomadic societies. Transformed into bold wayfarers, these nomads found a new existence with the horse: riding, packing, and trading, venturing farther and farther from home. Horses became prized possessions, and breeding superior steeds became a focus for many communities, particularly around the Mediterranean.

Ancient art proves that the spotted horse was highly valued in early civilizations. By the seventeenth century, spotted horses were popular as coach horses and mounts for King Louis XIV of France. By then spotted horses had become much sought-after for their beautiful color and refined elegance.

Spanish Horses in North America

The first spotted horses to reach North America are believed to have been shipped by the Spaniards. Spanish conquistadors, whose horses descended from stallions imported from the Mediterranean, plundered their way on horseback across the West Indies, Peru, and finally Mexico. One hundred years after Columbus visited the new land, the Spanish firmly established rule in Mexico, pasturing their horses in the rich grass prairies of the north. Tales of shiploads of spotted horses delivered to Mexico could account for those that eventually appeared in the American West.

In 1598 Philip II of Spain commissioned Juan de Oñate of New Spain, the area that now includes Mexico and Central America, to conquer and settle the upper valley of the Rio Grande. He and his men settled among villages of Pueblo Indians, who were forced to serve as serfs to farm the fields and herd the stock. If the peaceful Pueblos fled, they might face their even fiercer Apache, Comanche, Navajo, and Piute enemies.

Although Indians were not permitted to ride Spanish horses, many Indian stable boys secretly became experienced riders. Thus, if life became too difficult, they could

Mare and foal at Gramps Appaloosas, owned by Roy Scoles, Princeton, Idaho. Photo by Jason Abbott.

Proud Reflection, owned by Tom and Joanne O'Brien, Old River Ranch, Harvard, Idaho. Photo by Jason Abbott.

mount their horses and run far across the desert. Although runaways faced the danger of a worse fate outside their villages, some were adopted by other tribes and admired for their horses and horsemanship, which could earn them leadership status.

Spanish officials prohibited the sale of horses to the Indians. However, before long the Indians convinced the Spanish to trade horses for runaway slaves. In this way, the Plains tribes were able to build up their horse herds.

Indians and Appaloosas

The first recorded account of horses being utilized by western Indians was in the mid-17th century, and by 1680 Native tribes near Spanish settlements were using horses in their everyday lives. Resentment between the Pueblos and the Spanish continued to grow until the Indians of northern New Mexico finally rose up and killed hundreds of Spanish, driving the remainder far south. The horses that were confiscated from the Spanish were traded off to the Plains tribes, thus spreading the use of horses throughout the West over the next several decades.

Tribes native to the Plains relied on buffalo, making the horse a valuable hunting asset. Not only did the horse offer speed for the hunt, it could pack large quantities of meat and hides. In the Columbia Basin and eastern Oregon territory, however, Indians relied on salmon and other fish for their food supply, diminishing their need for pack animals or for speed. The area provided abundant forage and superior protection against raids, so horses were not needed for war and hunting.

The Cayuse, Palouse, and Nez Perce tribes developed horse-breeding programs and gradually improved the quality of their stock. Before long the Nez Perce became known for their sure-footed and reliable mounts, which served them well in the mountainous country of Oregon, Idaho, and Montana. Since women, children, and the elderly also used the horses, the horses' disposition was equally as important as their athleticism. Fractious, mean, or undesirable horses were quickly traded off, which explains the current Appaloosa's natural sagacity.

The Nez Perce also prized their spotted horse because of its smooth gait, sometimes called a running walk. This lateral gait, in which the legs on the same side of the horse move together, gives the rider a smooth, gliding ride. The motion of the horse is absorbed in its back and loins, providing fast-paced, low-to-the-ground movement.

The gait, first known to exist among the Spanish horses, was called "paso fino," which means "smooth-gaited." Originally the paso fino wasn't a breed of horse, but a characteristic gait prized for its natural quick pace. The North American paso fino horses were claimed by the Nez Perce and other tribes. This gait continues to be prized in such breeds as the Paso Fino, Peruvian Paso, Colombian Paso, and foundation-bred Appaloosa.

Ranchers and cowboys dubbed the smooth gait of the spotted horse the "Indian shuffle" and would pay more for a horse with the gait, since it saved wear and tear on the rider. Appaloosa Horse Club Hall of Fame inductee Robert L. Peckinpah wrote:

Rough country cowmen are unanimous, today, in praising the remarkable lack of leg trouble in this colorful, ground-covering horse. They are quick to point out that his natural traveling gait, the Indian shuffle, a seemingly tireless running walk, is a characteristic of this clean-legged horse in all but a few animals.

Gramps Appaloosas, owned by Roy Scoles, Princeton, Idaho. Photo by Jason Abbott.

The Indian shuffle is a huge asset to the endurance and trail horse. Many Appaloosa owners vow that this is one of the main reasons they own and breed foundation Appaloosa horses.

Because of the versatile lifestyle the horse offered, the Nez Perce tribe eventually split into two groups: those who hunted the plains for buffalo and those who remained in the basins to fish. The aristocrats of the nomadic Nez Perce tribe were honored with the most valued horses, which could run fast and follow an animal closely. The Nez Perce were always on the lookout for the fierce Blackfoot Indians, and quick war horses were also important for survival during battle.

Speed was an additional bonus, since the Indians loved horse racing and betting. A few devout Christian Nez Perce, however, may have had a negative attitude towards the horses because they were instrumental in both gambling and war, both sinful activities in the Christian mind.

The Palouse Horse Discovered

Lewis and Clark, during their westward expeditions, encountered the Northwest Indians' horses. A journal entry from Meriwether Lewis in 1806 reports:

Their horses appear to be of an excellent race; they are lofty, elegantly formed, active and durable; in short many of them look like fine English coarsers and would make a figure in any country. Some of those horses are pided [*sic*] with large spots of white irregularly scattered and intermixed with the black, brown, bey [*sic*] or some other color.

In 1855 Isaac Ingall Stevens, the territorial governor of Washington Territory, began an expedition east of Olympia to study various Indian tribes' lands and culture. He was also commissioned to gather information for a potential northern railroad line from the Pacific Coast to Mississippi.

Stevens floated up the Columbia River to Walla Walla, Washington, where he picked up the Nez Perce overland trail to the current-day Lewiston, Idaho, site on the Clearwater River.

CL Hart to Hart, "Lawyer," a Joker B. descendent. Owned by Vivian Knowles, Last Hurrah Ranch, Tensed, Idaho. Photo by Kevin Pullen.

Isaac's son, Hazard, upon discovering the rich land, recorded, "...and here I was astonished, not simply at the luxuriance of the grass, but the richness of the soil." Surrounded by rolling hills as far away as they could see, the group traveled for five days through the abundant countryside. On the second day they saw several hundred Nez Perce gathering camas roots, with around two thousand horses nearby. Stevens's group marveled at what they saw, went home and told others, and before long eager settlers invaded the area.

The War of 1877

As the white man fanned into the northwest Indian territory, the U.S. government signed a treaty with some of the Indians, setting aside specific lands for the tribes' ownership. After gold was discovered in Colville and Pierce, Idaho, in 1860, a new treaty was written in 1863, shrinking the reservation's size. Chiefs Joseph, Toohoolhoolzote, and White Bird refused to sign the new treaty, recognizing that they would be forced off their land. These tribes were called the nontreaty tribes, the largest led by young Chief Joseph. Chief Joseph and his tribe pastured their stock between the Wallowa Mountains and the Snake River Canyon in Oregon. As settlers flooded into Nez Perce tribe territory and conflicts over land rights ensued, war finally erupted in 1877. Chief Joseph heard of an ensuing attack by the U.S. Cavalry and gathered his people of all ages, nearly 1,000, plus some 1,800 head of stock for a hasty escape.

For more than three months the band eluded the cavalry, following a 1,300-mile trail through rough terrain all the way to Bear Paw, Montana. Many died along the mountain passes during these months of evasion. On September 29, 1877, the cavalry launched a surprise attack on the Nez Perce camp. After a six-day siege, tired, distraught, and filled with sorrow, Chief Joseph finally surrendered.

The U.S. Cavalry confiscated around 1,000 of the Nez Perce horses—those that had covered 1,300 miles of rough terrain in three and a half months. Some of the horses were taken to Fort Keogh and sold to buyers, and those that had remained on the open range were rounded up and used by cattlemen. Within 50 years, however, the spotted Indian horse became diluted and nearly extinct.

Mare and foal, Gramps Appaloosas, owned by Roy Scoles, Princeton, Idaho. Photo by Jessica Wright.

The Gift of a Horse

"His scalp-lock was tied with otter fur," Lieutenant Charles Erskine Scott Wood wrote of Chief Joseph on the day he surrendered to General Oliver Howard. "The rest of his hair hung in thick plaits on each side of his head. He wore buckskin leggings and a gray woolen shawl, through which were the marks of four or five bullets received in his last conflict. His forehead and wrist were also scratched by bullets," Wood recorded. ◆ Lieutenant Wood stood behind General Howard, taking mental notes to later write down what he saw and heard. His record of Chief Joseph's surrender speech has been repeated throughout history as one of the most dignified, heroic, and tragic speeches of all times. ◆ What C. E. S. Wood did not know that day was the profound impact the Nez Perce chief would have on his own life. ◆ The United States Cavalry had pursued Chief Joseph's band of Nez Perce Indians for nearly four months across 1,300 miles of rugged territory from the Wallowa Valley in Oregon to Bear Paw, Montana, close to the Canadian border. The battle had been long, the losses heavy, and the chief was weary with sorrow when he finally surrendered. Afterwards, his surviving people were exiled to Kansas and Oklahoma—far from their scenic homeland in eastern Oregon. The spotted horses that Chief Joseph and his band had bred for athleticism, beauty, and endurance were dispersed and eventually became nearly extinct. ◆ General Howard handed Lieutenant Wood charge of Chief Joseph, and the two developed a lasting friendship. Wood strove to right the wrongs done to the Nez Perce Indians

Leopard foal, Palisades Appaloosas, Lancaster, Kentucky.
Photo by owner Lisa Estridge.

Doncha Wanna Moon Me, owned by Tom and Kim Welch, TW Show Horses, Marysville, Ohio.
Photo by Brandy Segner.

Dreamin Dun, Palisades Appaloosas, Lancaster, Kentucky. Photo by Lisa Estridge.

by the United States. He helped Chief Joseph travel to Washington, D.C., to talk to Congress and was instrumental in getting him and his people back to the Northwest from their exile in the south. ◆ In July 1892, out of a deep respect for Chief Joseph, Wood sent his son, Erskine, to stay with the chief at his camp at the Nespelem Agency in Northeastern Washington to learn about Indian ways. The 12-year-old boy learned valuable lessons from Chief Joseph, and he eagerly went back the following summer. ◆ "Although I was just a boy, I knew that with Joseph I was living with a great man," Erskine recalled. "He was a father to me, guiding me in the Indian way of life." In an attempt to show his gratitude for what the chief had done, Charles Wood told Erskine to ask Chief Joseph if there was anything he could do for him in return for his kindness. ◆ "Give me a good stallion to improve the breed of my pony herd," the chief told Erskine. ◆ The request seemed too small and insignificant to Erskine. Why didn't he ask for his land back, he'd thought. Why didn't he ask to right the wrongs done to his people? Why a horse? What Erskine didn't fathom was the significance of horses to the Indians. The tribe had selectively bred them for decades and valued horses with the Appaloosa characteristics. "Why did I presume to decide for him what he should and should not do?" Erskine wrote years later, regretting that he never saw Chief Joseph again and that the chief's request had gone unfulfilled. ◆ As the years passed, Erskine married, had children and grandchildren, and often shared with them stories of his summers with Chief Joseph. "Until the day he died at age 104, Erskine Wood enjoyed recounting his days with Joseph to his children, grandchildren, great-grandchildren, and friends," said his granddaughter Mary Wood. ◆ Long after Charles, Erskine, and Chief Joseph died—105 years after Chief Joseph's request—Erskine's descendants decided to fulfill the chief's request for a good stallion. Family members donated money, and a worldwide search ensued for a magnificent Appaloosa stallion. At a ceremony in Joseph, Oregon, in July 1997, the 1994 stallion Zip's Wild Man by Nite Time Man and out of Zips Apache June was presented by Erskine's son, Erskine Biddle Wood, to Keith Soy Redthunder, Chief Joseph's oldest relative. ◆ "The gift of a horse is a wonderful thing," Redthunder said. ◆ Chief Joseph's Indian name was Hinmatooyalatkekt, interpreted as "thunder rolling over the mountains." As the family members left the site near Wallowa Lake following the 1997 ceremony, they claimed to hear the clap and roll of thunder across the magnificent, towering Wallowa Mountains.

Starting Over

Following the war of 1877, some Western ranchmen continued breeding Nez Perce horses for their own use. The horses worked well with cattle and were a hardy, trusted mount. Some highly colored Appaloosas entertained at circuses, enticing sweeping crowds. Soon came the Western spectacles headed by William Cody of Buffalo Bill's Wild West Show. A painting of Buffalo Bill Cody on his Appaloosa is included in a Western art collection at the Whitney Museum in Cody, Wyoming. He also owned a matched pair of Appaloosas that he used to pull a carriage.

After the circuses and the Wild West shows, roundups and rodeos became popular, often flaunting flashy Appaloosas. During this period, Charles Russell's Western art became popular, including a story in his 1927 book *Trails Plowed Under* that mentions the Nez Perce Appaloosa. Soon after, a story in *Western Horseman* magazine by historian Francis Haines featured an article about the Appaloosa, and the resulting fan mail authenticated a serious level of interest in the horse.

Mare and foal at Sheldak Ranch, Sheldon, North Dakota. Photo by owner Kim Utke.

Colt at open breed show, Princeton, Idaho. Photo by Kevin Pullen.

In December 1938, Claude Thompson of Moro, Oregon, started the Appaloosa Horse Club (ApHC) with six charter members. Claude felt a keen passion for preserving the unique Appaloosa and began a breeding effort to establish it as one of the most popular American breeds.

In September 1947, the ApHC moved its headquarters to Moscow, Idaho, where George Hatley became secretary. The first all-Appaloosa horse show took place in Lewiston, Idaho, in 1948. The club grew quickly under Hatley's leadership, and by the 1960s the Appaloosa had become a world favorite.

Now, as one of the most preferred breeds of horses in the United States, the Appaloosa has flourished, returning from near-extinction to prominence. But Appaloosa lovers don't just seek the color of the breed, even though it's a premium. Versatility in the show ring, endurance on the trail, speed on the racetrack, and human-like sensibility are other characteristics that breeders take pride in.

The Appaloosa has come a long way. Contemporary Appaloosa breeders look for color, sturdy sculpted conformation, and intelligence. For the Native Americans who still populate the Northwest, the horse has become an ideology, embodying the history of their people and the essence of the Palouse region: strong, rugged, durable, and stunningly gorgeous.

Blue Suede Dude, owned by Christy Wood. Heritage Class, 2006 Appaloosa National Show. Photo by Jennie Wandler.

Nature's Work of Art

Coats of Many Colors

Colour is my day-long obsession, joy and torment.

—Claude Monet

A colored Appaloosa is one of nature's most stunning works of art. Ornate, dramatic, elaborate—Appaloosas conjure up thoughts of Baroque period art with rich colors, graceful lines, and sculpted conformations. Or perhaps Fauvism comes to mind, an early 20th-century artistic movement that focused on bright, vibrant colors and bold brushwork—something like a halo-spotted blanket or leopard Appaloosa. More subtle tones are depicted in Surreal or Romantic art, creating a sense of calmness, like a blue or red roan Appaloosa.

Indeed, Appaloosas can display a wide variety of colorful art, including at least 13 different base coat colors, with various shades and hues of those colors, and seven accenting coat patterns. The Appaloosa color and coat pattern combinations that result are endless. Add in other variables, such as facial and leg markings and a range of colored manes and tails, and you will find each Appaloosa a distinctly colorful individual. Whether your artistic taste is orderly and defined, flashy and ornate, rich and rococo, or vivid and luminous, there is an Appaloosa that exhibits your preferred style.

Leopard gelding owned by Roy Scoles, Gramps Appaloosas, Princeton, Idaho. Photo by Jason Abbott.

My Dream

When I was very young, I had a dream one night of colored horses with spots that sparkled on their hips like fireworks on a black-sky canvas. Several of them grazed together in a rolling field, purpled with camas and set against a backdrop of craggy, snowcapped mountains. Drawn by the horses' vibrant beauty, I floated over the mountain meadow and straddled the back of a blue roan mare. My thighs were warmed against her smooth back and my eyes were cast in awe upon her spotted mates: palominos, leopards, buckskins, blacks—all with such intense colors that, out of my dream state, I still cannot describe them.   I recall feeling very peaceful as I ran my fingertips through the mare's silky mane and felt the aura of the horses' silent communication with each other. I felt I belonged in this place of color, and feared that the dream would end and I would lose the magical sensation of oneness with these majestic animals. Then, just when I believed my presence in the herd had gone entirely unnoticed, the mare lifted her head and gazed into my future.   When I awoke, I was never the same. I began to paint with swirling, vibrant colors and to write poems—and to ride Appaloosa horses.

Appaloosa owners love works of art, which is one of the reasons they possess one—or a whole herd. Although it's not *just* the color that draws horse-lovers to Appaloosas, color certainly makes the job of raising Appaloosas rich and intriguing.

When it comes to good horses, color is one of the defining characteristics that lifts the Appaloosa above other breeds into a league of its own. Let's explore some of the possibilities and dip into the elegant, artistic world of Appaloosa colors and characteristics.

Art evokes the mystery without which the world would not exist.

—RENÉ MAGRITTE

Suspicious Image, owned by Katie Burt of Spokane, Washington. Photo by Kevin Pullen.

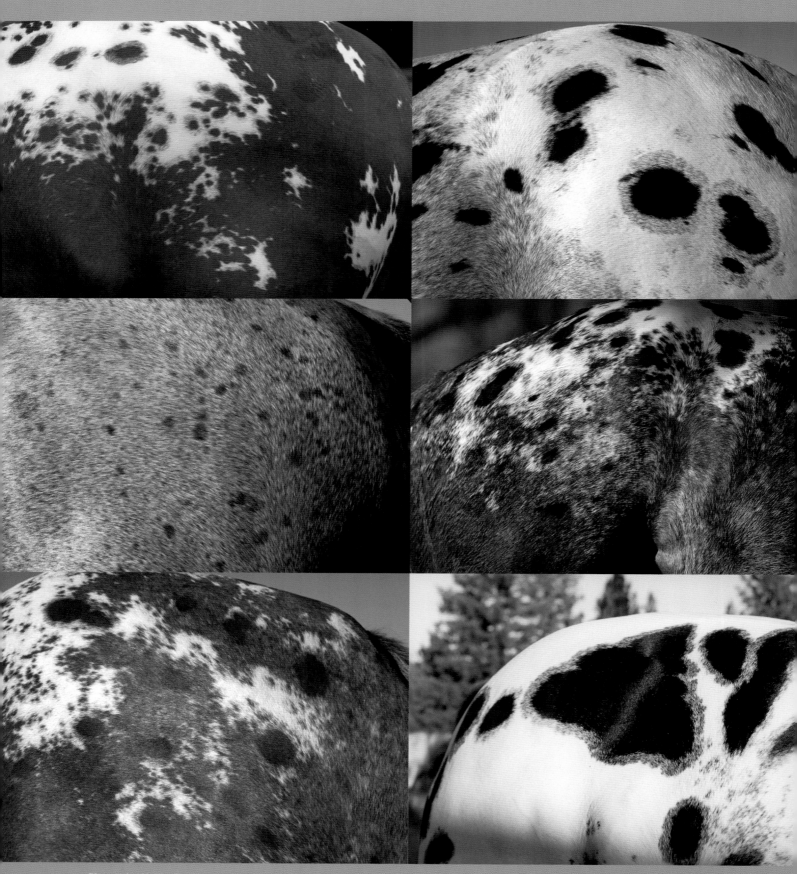

Photos by Kevin Pullen.

Award-winning sire The Hunter, owned by Doug and Sue Schembri, Char-O-Lot Ranch, Myakka City, Florida. Photo by owner Sue Schembri.

The classic defining characteristic of an Appaloosa is a blanket—that white splash that varies in size from a few flecks to a huge spread that extends from the tail to the withers and sometimes up the neck. Within the snowy patch of white may be darker, base-coat-colored spots. One of the most pleasing characteristics of Appaloosa spots is the surrounding lighter-colored hairs that lend a haloed, peacock look to the spots.

It is not always easy to predict the color an Appaloosa will eventually become from its coloring as a foal. Most foals are born with light-colored coats that become darker, with the exception of gray horses, which are born dark and become progressively lighter. The excitement of watching Appaloosa foal colors transform keeps breeders anticipating each year, with a renewed sense of astonishment at the outcome.

Although some Appaloosas are solid-colored, they still exhibit the other unique breed characteristics that set them apart: mottled skin, striped hooves, and visible sclera. Even if a foal is born solid-colored, it may develop a coat pattern later

Colorful foals, Sheldak Ranch, Sheldon, North Dakota. Photo by owner Kim Utke.

on. White hair intermingled with the base coat color is also common among Appaloosas, the reason why many Appaloosas become whiter with age.

There's always an element of mystery in breeding Appaloosas. Some breeders have even been surprised to mate two solid-colored horses and get an unexpected spotted foal. Many spotted Appaloosa stallions are bred to solid-colored mares in hopes of producing a spotted foal.

Let's take a look at the three distinctive characteristics besides coat patterns that adorn an Appaloosa. Once these characteristics are explained, we'll look into the many artistic coat patterns.

Proud Reflection, a Dreamfinder grandson, owned by
Tom and Joanne O'Brien, Old River Ranch, Harvard, Idaho.
Photo by Jason Abbott.

Tobys Spot Carlito, owned and photographed by Monika Hannawacker, Germany.

Art should astonish, transmute, transfix.

—BRETT WHITELEY

Distinct Characteristics

The three defining Appaloosa characteristics on horses that don't display a coat pattern, and on some that do, are mottled skin, visible sclera, and vertical-striped hooves. *Mottled skin* is unique to the Appaloosa horse and is a basic and decisive indicator of a true Appaloosa if no coat pattern is present. Mottled skin is pink or white intermixed with areas of darker, usually gray, pigmented skin. The result is a freckled or speckled pattern of pigmented and non-pigmented skin. Mottled skin can appear around the eyes, muzzle, and genitals of the Appaloosa.

Sclera is the white area of the eye that surrounds the iris, the center, colored portion of the eye. All horses have sclera, but the Appaloosa's is usually prominent and

Tobys Spot Carlito, owned and photographed
by Monika Hannawacker, Germany.

more visible than other breeds, giving the Appaloosa
an expressive, human-like gaze.

Many Appaloosas have bold and clearly defined
vertical-striped hooves that can occur in the absence
of white leg markings. However, stripes can occur on
other breeds as well, so striped hooves do not neces-
sarily distinguish Appaloosas from non-Appaloosas.
Therefore, it is important to identify other Appaloosa
characteristics in a horse with striped hooves.

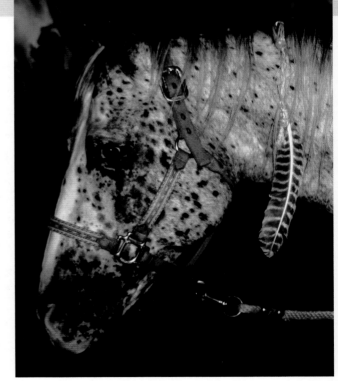

Indian decorated horse. Photo by Kristen Reiter.

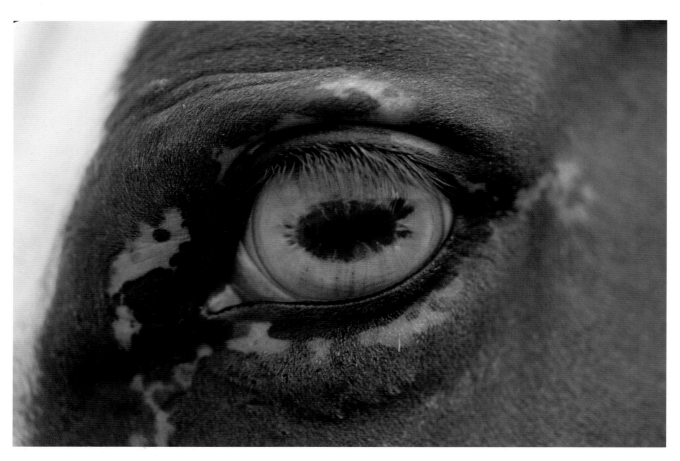

Mottling around the eye is a distinctly Appaloosa characteristic. Photo by Kevin Pullen.

Coat Patterns

The base coat, or background color behind any of the Appaloosa coat patterns, covers an entire range of color, including bay, dark bay, black, buckskin, grulla (blue-gray), dun, palomino, cremello or perlino (pale colored), chestnut, gray, bay roan, blue roan, and red roan.

Appaloosa coat patterns are highly variable, and some may not seem to fit into any category. Appaloosas generally exhibit about seven different coat patterns—from small spots that sprinkle the entire body to huge halo spots that seem to pop up from a striking white blanket.

Other interesting characteristics can accent the coat patterns of the Appaloosa, and there are a variety of nicknames for these. *Varnish marks* consist of a concentration of darker hairs mixed with a few white hairs that are usually found on the face, ears, knees, elbows, girth, stifle, hocks, hips, and flanks. They commonly occur on leopards and roans with few spots.

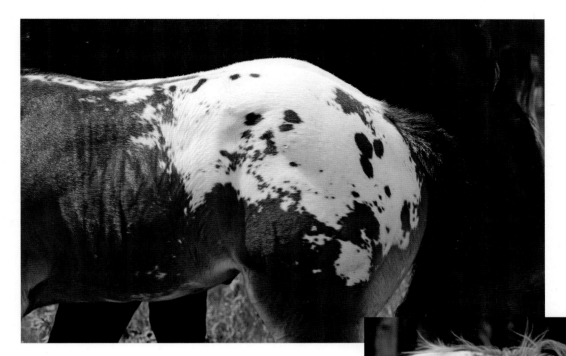

Striking blanket. Sheldak Ranch, Sheldon, North Dakota. Photo by owner Kim Utke.

Marbling occurs when there are varied areas of spots and speckles that give a lacy, slightly blotchy, or marbled appearance to the Appaloosa coat.

Frosting is a sprinkling of white hairs over the hips. It is commonly seen in the foal coat of an animal that later roans out.

Lightning marks occur on the legs, usually below the knee or hock, making the legs look striped. Lightning marks are caused by spots that merge together to form dark stripes against a white background.

Head to head color. Sheldak Ranch, Sheldon, North Dakota. Photo by owner Kim Utke.

Snowcaps to Lace Blankets

Blanketed Appaloosas wear one of the most popular and colorful of all the coat patterns. A blanket coat pattern consists of a solid white area normally over, but not limited to, the hip area that contrasts a darker base coat color. The white blanket can drape nearly

Foal at Sheldak Ranch, Sheldon, North Dakota. Photo by owner Kim Utke.

CL Hart to Hart by Cherry's Leader, out of Scottish Maid. Owned by Vivian Knowles, Last Hurrah Ranch, Tensed, Idaho. Photo by Kevin Pullen.

Doncha Wanna Moon Me, owned by Tom and Kim Welch, TW Show Horses, Marysville, Ohio.
Photo by Brandy Segner.

the entire body of the horse, or it may cover just the hips. A blanket that covers more than the hips and loins is called an extended blanket.

Some blankets are solid and without spots, called "snowcaps." Other blankets are splashed with large halo spots, and some have a sprinkling of small spots. The "lace" blanket is restricted to the rump, and is intermixed with base-coat-colored hairs, particularly around the edges. Often the lace blanketed Appaloosa will roan out completely, giving it the appearance of a few-spot leopard or roan.

Some Hall of Fame Appaloosas with spectacular blankets were Patchy, Bright Eyes Brother, Top Hat H., and Chief Of Four Mile. Many descendants of these famous Appaloosas have carried on not just their talents, but their striking blankets as well.

1996 Hall of Fame stallion Dreamfinder had an extended blanket part way up his neck, with large brilliant chestnut spots. Many of his progeny carry his striking color.

Spots of All Shapes

Dark spots that occur on a white or light background can vary in size from flecks to larger spots of more than 10 centimeters in diameter. The spots are usually round

Head to foot spots. Photo by Kevin Pullen.

or oval, but may be irregular when two or more spots overlap. They can also form interesting shapes, like hearts. Spots may occur in large numbers and dense clusters or be very sparsely scattered over the horse. Sometimes the hair in the spots is longer or shorter than the surrounding coat hair.

One of the most popular spotted coat patterns, called a leopard, distinguishes these loud-colored Appaloosas from other breeds. Leopards, who have a white or light-colored base coat with darker spots over the entire body, exhibit one of the most spectacular coat patterns of all Appaloosas and are highly sought after by some breeders.

Some Hall of Fame leopard Appaloosas are Prince Plaudit, Double Six Domino, and High Sign. One famous Hall of Fame leopard stallion named Sundance

Tobys Spot Carlito, owned and photographed by Monika Hannawacker, Germany.

Proud Reflection, owned by Tom and Joanne O'Brien, Old River Ranch, Harvard, Idaho.
Photo by Jason Abbott.

Leopard gelding owned by Roy Scoles, Gramps Appaloosas, Princeton, Idaho. Photo by Jason Abbott.

had a bright white body with deep chestnut spots. His coat was so beautiful that when he died of colic in 1955, his owners preserved his hide.

Tom and Joanne O'Brien of Old River Ranch near Harvard, Idaho, own a leopard Dreamfinder grandson named Proud Reflection who sired three full sisters, all with distinctly different colors and coat patterns: solid-colored, blanketed, and frosted roan.

Hi Tech Cowboy, owned by Brian Amerine and Amy Kocher, Sycamore Run Appaloosas, Ohio, is another popular leopard stallion who consistently sires performance and halter prospects with color and athletic conformation. Hi Tech Cowboy, by Dreamfinder and out of Impress A Cowboy, has tested homozygous for black, which means that he will not sire red foals regardless of the color of the dam.

Roans of All Colors

The roan Appaloosa coat exhibits different hues of base-coat-colored hairs intermingled with white hairs. Roaning can develop from any base color except white, but lighter colors like duns and palominos are not as common as black, dark brown, chestnut, or sorrel. Roaning may begin as early as the shedding of the baby hair, or

Classy, owned by John and Julie Kreider of Sawyer Creek Appaloosas, Gouverneur, New York.
Photo by Jillian Paige Dunkleberger.

as late as 10 years or more. The roan Appaloosa's face generally has fewer white hairs than its body, but lighter hair color around the eyes, elbows, and/or flanks may signify that a base color roaning will eventually occur.

Roans generally show all of the Appaloosa characteristics: parti-colored skin, striped hooves, and white sclera. Mix in a multi-colored mane and tail, and you have a spectacular colored horse. Most roan-colored Appaloosas will become whiter over the years, and Appaloosa roans will generally show varnish marks as well.

Roan blanketed Appaloosas have a roan base coat with a blanket that usually covers the hip area, but sometimes covers more. The white blanket can be a solid snowcap, or can have spots of various sizes.

Many Hall of Fame Appaloosas were roans, including racehorse legends Apache Double, It's Golden Girl—a famous racehorse and producer of several champion racing colts and fillies—and Perfect One, a 1979 mare who also raced and went on to produce 14 racing foals.

Foal owned by Roy Scoles, Gramps Appaloosas, Princeton, Idaho. Photo by Jason Abbott.

Solid Colored

Solid Appaloosas have a base color but no contrasting Appaloosa coat pattern. What distinguishes this horse as an Appaloosa is mottled skin plus sclera or striped hooves. About one-third of all Appaloosas born are solid-colored, presenting a peculiar problem for a horse breed known for color. While genetic researchers continue to seek solutions to this problem, breeders accept the fact that there are no guarantees they will always get a spotted foal.

One famous solid-colored Appaloosa is 1998 Hall of Fame mare Skip The Color. "Color" is a solid dun mare who was crossed with many leading Appaloosa sires, including Dreamfinder and Impressive Andrew. She produced numerous winning halter foals.

Taking a bow. Sheldak Ranch, Sheldon, North Dakota. Photo by owner Kim Utke.

Impressive Andrew, who was inducted into the Hall of Fame in 1997 and died in 2001, produced 356 registered foals that have earned numerous show medallions—most excelled at halter. Impressive Andrew was exactly that—an impressive solid black stallion.

Breeders' Passion

Appaloosa breeders are outspoken about the reasons they have chosen this breed above all others. Donna Shaffer of Shaffer's Appaloosa Acres in Winterset, Iowa, says, "We started raising Appaloosas in 1967 because of their unique coat patterns. The most rewarding part of breeding is to take your colorful horses into the show pen and to compete and win at any level. Just think of the satisfaction of raising an

Appaloosa, taking it to the World Show, and winning. It's an experience we wish everyone could have."

Donna and her husband, Ron, have a room full of trophies and ribbons to signify their winning breeding program. Their horses boast some of the best winning bloodlines in the business and have competed and won at both the national and world levels. Their 1998 stallion, This Mr Has It All, is a multiple National champion–producing Appaloosa. With bloodlines that go back to Bright Eyes Brother and Glamour Bars, this stallion has produced numerous halter champions.

Now retired from showing, Ron and Donna continue to anticipate a new foal crop every year, and they feel a deep sense of pride watching those foals go to good homes and on to the show ring to win.

Some breeders wait years before they get what they consider the "perfect" Appaloosa specimen, like Rex Kennard of Yukon, Oklahoma. When Rex first saw his brilliant-colored Appaloosa foal sired by Alias King and out of the mare Aztec's Fancy Frani in 1984, there was no doubt this was the foal he and his wife had saved the name "Dreamfinder" for. The brilliant foal went on to capture the essence of the Appaloosa breed and pass his incredible color, elegance, and personality to his progeny.

"I don't know that there's ever been an Appaloosa stallion—or ever will be—that will make his mark on the breed like he did," Roger Perry, Dreamfinder's last owner, says. "When his babies hit the ground, they went to the show pen. He changed the look of the Appaloosa breed."

"He's been the horse that impacted our breed the most," says Mayra Orihuela of Alejo Appaloosas in Moorpark, California, who owned four mares by Dreamfinder. "He brought color, balance, and beauty. He was an eye catcher, and he won people's hearts. He became everyone's horse. Anybody that ever had anything to do with him—if you just looked him in the eye—he was a part of your life forever. He was very, very special."

Dreamfinder was inducted into the Appaloosa Horse Club Hall of Fame in 1996 and died in 2002. Statistically, he's already laid claim as one of the greatest Appaloosa sires of all time, but the impact of his legacy is yet to be fully realized.

Foal at Sheldak Ranch, Sheldon, North Dakota. Photo by owner Kim Utke.

Art washes away from the soul the dust of everyday life.

—PABLO PICASSO

Everyone has his or her own personal favorites when it comes to Appaloosa coat patterns. Picasso fans might be drawn to the bright splashes of color on the leopard or blanketed Appaloosas, while Monet fans might choose the roans and more muted colors. But you don't have to be an art connoisseur to recognize that the Appaloosa horse is a living, breathing work of nature's most dramatic art. Add in warm personalities, gentle temperaments, and amazing athleticism, and you have an animal anyone would be proud to own.

Leopard foals, Palisades Appaloosas, Lancaster, Kentucky. Photo by owner Lisa Estridge.

Dream in Color

Breeding Appaloosas

There is something about breeding good horses that makes it the Sport of Kings.

—Stanley Harrison

In conversations with George Hatley in 1946 and 1947, Sam Fisher, a half-Nez Perce and half-Palouse Indian, became highly enthusiastic when he talked about the "medicine" used for breeding good Appaloosas. Sam was from the family of Nez Perce occupying land north of the Snake River. This band is considered by some to be a separate tribe, referred to as the Palouse Indians. Because they were not part of Chief Joseph's band, it is doubtful that any of their people joined in the war of 1877. Thus their horse herds remained intact.

JW, owned by John and Julie Kreider, Sawyer Creek Appaloosas, Gouverneur, New York.
Photo by Jillian Paige Dunkleberger.

Colorful foal, Sheldak Ranch, Sheldon, North Dakota. Photo by owner Kim Utke.

Sam claimed that the Indians performed a ritual for each mare during at least two stages of pregnancy to ensure a nicely marked Appaloosa foal. First, he said, you should mate the most desirable mare with the most desirable stallion. He then gestured by putting his fingertips together with his arms about six inches from his belt to describe a mare showing the first signs of being with foal. This was followed by gestures and descriptions in Nez Perce of the ritual the mare was put through. Then he said, "Just before mare have colt," and made a wide circle with his arms indicating the final stages of pregnancy, followed by the gestures and descriptions of the second ritual the mare was to go through to ensure a well-marked foal. He concluded by saying, "If everything right—it work."

George was interested to know to what extent the Nez Perce Indians differentiated the Appaloosas from other horses and wanted to know if there was a word in

Broodmares, Sheldak Ranch, Sheldon, North Dakota. Photo by owner Kim Utke.

their language for Appaloosa. "This was a rather difficult task because, although Sam Fisher could understand and speak some English, he didn't understand why we wanted a Nez Perce word for something we were both using the commonly used word for," George said. "But we were finally successful. The Nez Perce word for Appaloosa is *Maumin*, pronounced Ma-meen. The Nez Perce word for the Paint or pinto horse is *Tam-sel-peen*, showing that the two horses were not confused with one another."

By the end of the 19th century, the American spotted horses were sparse, and it was difficult to return the breed to its original foundation bloodlines. Although a few Appaloosas had been traded and spread throughout the West, there were no known

Shannon Utke with Hall of Fame
Appaloosa Prince Shannon, 1974.
Sheldak Ranch, Sheldon, North Dakota.
Photo by owner Kim Utke.

Hanna, owned by John and Julie
Kreider of Sawyer Creek Appaloosas,
Gouverneur, New York. Photo by
Jillian Paige Dunkleberger.

breeding programs in place to preserve the Appaloosa's uniqueness. Thus, by the time the Appaloosa Horse Club began its quest in 1938 to preserve the breed, few original foundation Appaloosas could be found.

It was apparent that Appaloosas needed to be crossed with other breeds in order to be re-established. In the early days of the Appaloosa Horse Club, breeders seldom kept written records of their breeding program, and any horses that had unidentified parentage but that displayed Appaloosa characteristics could be registered. By the mid-1970s, however, the books were closed to all outside breeding except to registered Arabians, Quarter Horses, and Thoroughbreds—a rule that continues to this day.

In describing the relative value of the Appaloosa in comparison to other horses in language we could all understand, the Indian said, "One Appalousy—one truckload of other horses."

—GEORGE HATLEY, IN SPEAKING OF HIS CONVERSATIONS WITH SAM FISHER

The race. Palisades Appaloosas, Lancaster, Kentucky. Photo by owner Lisa Estridge.

Reserve National Champion Awestruck, Sheldak Ranch, Sheldon, North Dakota. Photo by owner Kim Utke.

Early Legends

To understand the heritage and lineage of the early Appaloosas that made up the first ApHC registry, we'll look at a few famous foundation horses and their breeders. There are, however, numerous foundation Appaloosas responsible for current day bloodlines.

The Circus Horse and Primero

Owned by Coke Roberds

Near the turn of the 20th century, Coke Roberds, a rancher and horse breeder from Colorado, bred a stallion, purchased from a nearby circus and called The Circus Horse, to a racing mare. What resulted was a colorful spotted stallion that Roberds named Arab. Roberds later purchased a Thoroughbred chestnut stallion named Primero that he bred to some of the solid-colored mares produced by Arab. Their get were foals with Appaloosa characteristics. Unfortunately, Primero was killed in an accident while he was being shipped from Oklahoma to Colorado, but one roan Appaloosa daughter of Primero survived. She was later bred to an AQHA foundation stallion and produced the blue roan mare that produced Joker B.

Joker B., 1941-1966

Owned by Carl Miles

Foaled in 1941, Joker B. seemed like a genetic phenomenon, but his lineage traced back to Coke Roberds's breeding era. He was sired by a registered Quarter Horse and out of an unregistered blue roan mare from Roberds—the grandaughter of Primero. To everyone's surprise, Joker B. was born with a large white blanket covered by plenty of black spots. Jack Casement, who owned Joker B., gave the stallion as a gift to his wife, who subsequently sold him to a neighbor. After being sold to several other owners, Joker B. ended up with Bill Benoist, who incorporated him into his breeding program using some of the best mares. In 1959 Joker B. was purchased by wealthy Texas oilman Carl Miles for $10,000, and promoted extensively.

CL Hart to Hart, "Lawyer," a Joker B. descendent. Owned by Vivian Knowles, Last Hurrah Ranch, Tensed, Idaho. Photo by Kevin Pullen.

CL Hart to Hart, "Lawyer," a Joker B. descendent. Owned by Vivian Knowles, Last Hurrah Ranch, Tensed, Idaho. Photo by Kevin Pullen.

Miles bred Joker B. to his finest mares, producing numerous champions who went on to produce their own champions. Joker B. was inducted into the Appaloosa Hall of Fame in 1988.

Red Eagle, 1946-1971

Owned by Claude Thompson

After Claude Thompson founded the Appaloosa Horse Club, he launched an effort to breed the Appaloosa back to its original athletic conformation. He began by breeding his stocky Appaloosa mares to a 1932 Arabian stallion named Ferras, who had been imported from England and was famous for producing high-quality horses.

In 1945 Thompson bred Ferras to the mare Painter's Marvel, a granddaughter of Ferras. Her colt, Red Eagle, became a show champion and a sire of champions. Red Eagle was a bay with spots, and in 1951 he was named the National Champion Appaloosa stallion. After his show career, Red Eagle was sold to actor John Derek to be featured in a film that never transpired. Later he was sold to Thomas Clay of Caliente, Nevada, where Red Eagle sired 81 foals. Several became National champions and quality breeding stock.

Wapiti, 1955-1979

Owned by Jim Wild

In 1955 a stallion with all the Appaloosa characteristics was born to two solid-colored registered Quarter Horses, Gold Heels and Cuadroon. The stallion was named Wapiti, and some believed him to be a genetic freak. But his pedigree revealed something interesting—that Quarter Horses and Appaloosas shared some foundation pedigrees. Wapiti's parentage derived from two solid-colored registered Quarter Horses who had recessive color genes. Wapiti placed in the top three at the National Show's get of sire class from 1968 to 1970. He sired 220 registered foals, many who became National and World champions. Wapiti died in 1979 of cancer and is buried under a life-size statue of himself.

Dawndee, 1959-1990

Owned by Glade Draper

Racing Hall of Fame mare Dawndee, a foundation-bred Appaloosa, became the first AAA-rated Appaloosa mare. She held her own in races against Quarter Horses and Thoroughbreds and set a world record in 1966 at Brush, Colorado. Dawndee started her race career as a 2-year-old, but was then taken off the track to breed. While in foal, she was put back to work and subsequently carried several foals to term during her race career, including Racing Hall of Fame sprint colt War Don. One of her daughters, Camee Dee, produced Bold Concept, a five-time Gold Invitational Handicap winner.

Dawndee produced 11 foals, seven of who made starts at the track and five who went on to win. Dawndee was euthanized at 31 years old because of failing health.

A Legendary Breeder

Some early breeders stand out above the others, and their stories are worth retelling over and over again. George Hatley first recorded the following story in 1954—a testimony to the hardships and joys of one well-known Palouse Appaloosa breeder. ◆ *Having produced over 300 head of Appaloosas, no one person was as widely known in the Palouse country for his horses as Floyd Hickman. Floyd always did like Appaloosas, but his breeding program didn't develop until he rode his red roan Appaloosa mare, Spot, 40 miles down the Snake River to Central Ferry to breed her to Chet Lamb's well-known Appaloosa stallion Knobby. He made the ride, and the next year his mare foaled, but the foal was sired by a young half draft stallion Chet had used to tease the mare. The draft stallion had gotten to the mare while Floyd was in the house. During those years, service fees were not collected until the mare dropped her foal. "I not only got a colt I didn't want," Floyd said, "but I also had to pay the service fee, because she did have a colt."* ◆ *The next year another ride was made to Central Ferry. The following year Spot foaled a fine stud colt they named Dan, who proved to be an excellent foundation sire. He was black in front with patches of black on his white loin and hips. Dan weighed between 950 and 1,000 pounds and stood around 14:3. He was a good traveler and a fine stock horse.* ◆ *Spot was very gentle and had a good disposition—the children later rode her to school. Floyd placed a premium on the Appaloosa's good disposition.* ◆ *The Hickman family was expecting guests on Christmas Eve, 1924. In order to have a Christmas tree for the children, Floyd got on his horse and rode to an abandoned farmstead to cut the top of a tree when the brittle, frozen limbs snapped. Floyd fell, crushing his right knee. A strong west wind with the mercury at eight below zero gave him little hope of surviving until someone came. A fence separated him and his horse, so he pulled himself backward by his hands to the door of the old shack. The door was frozen shut, so he tried to cut around it with his pocketknife. The blade broke.* ◆ *He would have probably frozen there at the door had it not been for his children's dog. The dog had been coddled by the children, even being rocked in a doll cradle, so Floyd called the dog up to him and held him close to his chest. He was found by a brother, Clare, and an uncle, Elmer Hickman, who saw*

Tobys Spot Carlito, owned and photographed by Monika Hannawacker, Germany.

that he could not be moved on horseback, so one of them rode to neighbor's, Clay Barr, for a sled. The men were not long getting back to him with the sled and a pint of whiskey. He emptied the bottle; and after they got him home, the doctor arrived and administered enough morphine to put two ordinary men to sleep. Evidently the two types of painkiller did not react well, as he was pretty violent for a few days. It took nearly three weeks to slowly thaw the crushed leg. Toward spring, his leg was amputated near the hip. The first thing he said to Dr. Bryant after coming out of the anesthetic was, "Will I be able to ride?" ◆ *"You'll be able to ride a horse" the doctor assured him. "It's your left leg that counts." Floyd did ride—about five years later he won a keg race, which demands fast dismounting, at the county fair.* ◆ *Floyd's second sire was Old Blue, who was sired by Dan and out of a mare named Lucy bred by Sam Fisher.*

Lucy was a red roan Appaloosa that stood around 15:1 and weighed around 1,100 pounds. When Floyd first bought Lucy, she had a filly at her side that was chestnut with large white spots over the loin and hips. Both were kept as broodmares as long as they lived. ◆ *Old Blue had the most use as a sire of any of Floyd Hickman's stallions. Old Blue was black with white over the loin and hips and later turned blue in front. He was foaled around 1930; at maturity he stood about 15:2 and weighed around 1,100 pounds. He was very well put together and was undoubtedly the most popular sire in the Palouse country, judging from the demand for his service. During one year, Old Blue stood to 109 mares outside his own band. The following year he was paid for 77 foals; some were never paid for.* ◆ *The third stallion in Floyd Hickman's program was Toby I. He was a smooth, attractive horse who also stood about 15:2 and weighed around 1,100 pounds. He was a dark blue roan, white with black spots over the loin and hips. He was sired by Old Blue around 1935 and was out of an Appaloosa mare named Trixie. Trixie carried the brand of a man named Lee who lived at Dayton, Washington. Trixie had an exceptionally fast getaway and was raced considerably in relay races in the Northwest. She was considered by Floyd to be one of the best broodmares he ever owned. Her foals proved her value, because out of 14 foals, only one, which was wire cut, brought less than $100. More than $100 during hard times was good money for a horse.* ◆ *When Trixie became too old to rough it during the winter, she was given to a cousin of Floyd's who raised two or three additional foals. She was about 27 years old when I saw her. She was a bit more angular, due some to age, than most Appaloosas, and weighed around 1,050 pounds, standing 15:1. She was a dark red roan in front, white with chestnut spots over the loin and hips. In asking Floyd about her racing, he said she was loaned out every fall for several years to some people who made the circuit to all the county fairs and races in the area. Then he sort of grinned and said, "I suppose the best thing you could say about her speed and getaway was that during prohibition a bootlegger used her to deliver bottled whiskey."* ◆ *Floyd considered Toby I the best stock horse he ever owned. He was a handy rope horse and really tops for cutting. Floyd said, "You could go into a herd and cut out what you wanted and put it where you wanted it—you didn't have to think for him." Toby I was a versatile horse and competed and won in about every* kind of performance class made. He constantly won the working stock horse classes at Sandpoint, Idaho, and neighboring shows. At the First National Appaloosa Show at Lewiston, Idaho, in 1948, he was the top money winner of the show. After this show, he was retired. ◆ There are many reasons why people like Appaloosas. Floyd likes them for their performance, temperament, and disposition. Floyd said, "You could get one, ride him five or six times, and sell him as green broke. That's not the way with a lot of horses—they require a professional trainer and a year's training. Appaloosas have feet and legs that stand up in the rocks, and they know how to handle themselves in the breaks and canyons." Floyd stayed on his Appaloosa regardless of how steep the country and how narrow the trails. A man who used to ride with him in the rough country said, "Whenever Floyd would free his wooden leg from the stirrup, I'd get off and lead my horse. I know I'd be safer afoot than mounted."

Open breed show, Caldwell, Idaho. Photo by Jeri Rainer.

Dream in Color

Ready Dream Dust, owned and photographed by Monika Hannawacker, Germany.

Contemporary Bloodlines

Contemporary Appaloosa breeding has become more of a science. With the technology to freeze and ship semen, it is possible to breed mares to a select stallion anywhere in the world. And although current-day breeders don't perform any standard rituals to ensure a colored foal, they do try to find a stallion and dam that are known to pass on Appaloosa color, easygoing temperaments, and athletic conformations to their foals. Some breeders have found perfect combinations, but predicting a foal's color has yet to become an exact science.

Through selective breeding by men determined to restore the magnificent Appaloosa as a breed, the horse was on its way to becoming the recognized, high-quality animal that it had once been. Through the descendents of these foundation Appaloosa champions there eventually developed two different types of Appaloosas: those who maintained foundation bloodlines as much as possible by breeding Appaloosa to Appaloosa, and those crossed with other breeds, most often to be used as show horses in halter classes.

Dreamin Dun, Palisades Appaloosas, Lancaster, Kentucky. Photo by Lisa Estridge.

The Appaloosa Horse Club recognizes the value of foundation-bred Appaloosas through its Generation Advancement Program and Foundation Pedigree Designation, which identify and reward horses with bloodlines that are a result of Appaloosa-to-Appaloosa breeding.

Some contemporary Appaloosas have made their mark on the Appaloosa breed like no other. Following are a few of those special horses that will never be forgotten.

Hi Tech Cowboy, owned by Sycamore Run Appaloosas, LLC; Delaware, Ohio. Photo by Jillian Paige Dunkleberger.

Prince Plaudit, 1963-1988

Owned by Carl Miles

Carl Miles purchased Prince Plaudit after Joker B. passed away in 1966. Prince Plaudit was foaled in 1963 and had a pedigree that traced back to AQHA foundation sire Old Fred. Miles was convinced that his new stallion would continue where Joker B. left off. He was right. After winning multiple championships, Prince Plaudit was sold at an auction in 1974 for $260,000. Soon after, he was syndicated for $300,000. In 1988 he was inducted into the Appaloosa Horse Club's Hall of Fame, the same year that he died of natural causes.

Apache Double, 1969-1999

Bred by George Hatley

Owned by Iola Hatley

Apache Double became the first $2 million producer in the history of Appaloosa racing. Inducted into the Appaloosa Horse Club Racing Hall of Fame in 2001, Apache Double, born on May 17, 1969, was a product of the Appaloosa mare Run Around

Famous racehorse Apache Double, owned by George and Iola Hatley. Photo courtesy of George and Iola Hatley.

and the Thoroughbred stallion Double Reigh. The stallion finished his racing career with a 21-18-3-0 record. At the 1975 National Show, he stood reserve champion out of 54 entries in aged stallion halter.

Apache Double also produced 422 foals that include 210 race starters and 134 winners. He died in 1999 at the age of 30.

Bright Zip, 1975-2003

Owned by John Lyons

John Lyons bought Bright Zip as a yearling from G. L. Barth of Holly, Colorado, after being introduced to the Appaloosa breed by his brother. As John developed his training style using the stallion, their relationship grew and the stallion gained national attention. Bright Zip was inducted into the Hall of Fame because of the revolutionary method of natural horsemanship that he and John developed.

In an interview with *Appaloosa Journal* in 1996, John said, "My relationship with him is as close to father-son as it can be. It's a relationship that goes beyond

John Lyons and Bright Zip. ©CharlesHilton.com

just horse and rider. It's a bond of dependence. When I've needed an extra-special tool, he's been that tool. When I've needed a special friend, he was that friend."

In 1995 Bright Zip lost his eyesight to a medical allergy, but continued performing at symposiums. He produced 21 foals in his lifetime. John saddled up Bright Zip for the last time when he married Jody Davini on June 7, 2003. The stallion was euthanized two months later.

Sir Wrangler, 1977-2006

Owned by Joe and Jan Bard

Sir Wrangler left a mark on everyone who met him. Born in 1977, he was a 15:2-hand, 1,150-pound bay roan with a large blanket and spots. Bred to any type of mare, Wrangler always produced horses with excellent minds and versatility that became lifelong family members to anyone who owned them. Wrangler's dominant traits were large, well-set eyes; great neck and shoulder angles; long croup; straight legs; and vee chest.

Sir Wrangler's progeny are successful in all facets of showing. In 1998 he was immortalized as a Breyer model, and later he was a guest of honor at many

John Lyons and Bright Zip. ©CharlesHilton.com

Doncha Wanna Moon Me, owned by Tom and Kim Welch, TW Show Horses, Marysville, Ohio.
Photo by Brandy Segner.

BreyerFests. One of his foals, a filly named Wild Bay Be Blues, was depicted with her dam on a U.S. postage stamp.

"Wrangler horses are seen from working cattle to mountain riding," says Jan Bard. "My best friend, Chris Nelson, and I have been spending two weeks every summer in the mountains for the last 25 years. Wrangler horses have gotten us out of many scary moments and places and have been the vehicle for making lasting friendships and memories."

Dreamfinder, 1984-2002

Bred by Rex Kennard

Dreamfinder, by Alias King and out of the Quarter Horse mare Aztecs Fancy Frani, exemplifies the perfect contemporary Appaloosa in every aspect: color, temperament,

Hall of Fame stallion Dreamfinder. Photo by Debbie Moors, courtesy of the Appaloosa Horse Club.

athleticism, and an amazing ability to pass these qualities on to his get. Dreamfinder made his mark on the Appaloosa industry like no other horse.

Rex Kennard, who bred Dreamfinder, sent him to Joan Santos Whitehouse as a weanling for showing. He never placed lower than first and often received grand or reserve grand champion in his class. After he went on to win the World Show, he was retired at Joan's California ranch as a stud for several years. Dreamfinder went on to produce numerous champions. Some of his accomplishments include:

- 1985 World Champion and National Grand Champion
- Ranked leading Appaloosa sire of point-earning halter-horse and halter-class winners
- The first yearling in history to be named National Grand Champion
- The first stallion to sire two National Grand Champions in the same year
- The youngest stallion to sire a World Champion

- Bronze Sire Production Plaque winner in halter
- The youngest stallion to win both the National Champion and World Champion Get of Sire title
- The youngest stallion ranked by the Appaloosa Horse Club as leading halter sire of the breed.

All Hands On Zip, 1992

Owned by Nancy Magnussen

Standing 17 hands, this Appaloosa stallion moves with the grace and power of a world champion. Sired by the Quarter Horse Zippo Jack Bar and Appaloosa mare

Award-winning sire The Hunter, owned by Doug and Sue Schembri, Char-O-Lot Ranch, Myakka City, Florida. Photo by owner Sue Schembri.

All Hands On Deck, All Hands On Zip has won several World, National, and Appaloosa Pleasure Horse Association titles.

As a talented show horse in hunter under saddle and western pleasure, All Hands On Zip is described as "poetry in motion." He ended his show career in 1999 to become a top producer of hunter under saddle and western pleasure futurity horses. His foals have inherited his size, color, and quiet-minded temperament, as well as his movement and high-class style.

The Hunter, 1993

Owned by Doug and Sue Schembri

Doug and Sue Schembri, who own Char-O-Lot Ranch in west central Florida, have won the prestigious Appaloosa Horse Club Leading Breeder award four times. They also won the Leading Breeder of Halter Horses title in 1997 and 1998 before it became the Leading Breeder title. They have produced and shown numerous National and World ApHC Champions in both halter and performance, in addition to preparing and exhibiting hundreds more for their clients. Char-O-Lot Ranch is home to The Hunter, who is the 2002, 2003, and 2004 Leading Sire of Appaloosa Performance Horses.

Maid For Show (2001-2005) and Phenomenal (2006)

Owned by John and Julie Kreider

"Maid For Show, or J.W., exceeded all our expectations," said Julie Kreider of Sawyer Creek Appaloosas in northern New York State. "Not only was he an exceptional-looking horse, he had that disposition that endeared everyone to him. We thought we would go into our old age with J.W., as he was the epitome of what we felt a breeding stallion should be: excellent conformation, keen athletic ability, superior pedigree, loud color and superb disposition.

"Unfortunately that was not the case. Our just-turned-4-year-old stallion died tragically of a heart attack, and our dreams went with him."

After losing J.W., Julie and her husband, John, began a search for a replacement stallion. Years earlier, the couple had tried to buy Judy Parlier's horse Spectravision, whom they felt was the best leopard Appaloosa mare in the industry. At three years old, after winning three bronze medallions and her National Championship,

Spectravision was bred and retired from the show ring. The pregnancy was difficult, and Spectravision ended up needing a cesarean section and losing her foal. Adding more tragedy, during the procedure they discovered the mare had multiple adhesions in her abdomen and would never be able to carry a foal.

Judy never gave up hope, though. After years of begging, she finally convinced her veterinarian to attempt an embryo transfer from Spectravision into a recipient mare, who would carry the foal to term.

Judy made arrangements to proceed and decided to breed Spectravision to a Quarter Horse. After careful research, she chose a stallion that she felt was the absolute best cross for her mare—a four-time AQHA World Champion, multiple AQHA World Champion producer, and Congress Grand Champion stallion Call Me Phenomenal.

The veterinarian flushed an embryo from Spectravision on the first try, and the embryo took in the selected recipient Paint mare. As the pregnancy progressed, everyone laughed at the idea of seeing an Appaloosa foal born to a mare with the wrong kind of spots.

On February 9, 2006, a red leopard colt was born to a Paint mare. Not only did he have great color, he was a grand-looking little guy and quickly became the talk of the town.

"Though grief stricken over the loss of J.W., John and I immediately noticed how truly special this new red leopard colt was," Julie says. "He is the only Appaloosa offspring of the Quarter Horse Call Me Phenomenal and of the great mare, Spectravision. It didn't take us long to see that this very special colt had all the qualities we sought after and could take over our program where J.W. left off," Julie adds.

"The rest is up to fate. Our goal is to breed and produce the highest quality Appaloosas, with emphasis on leopards. In order to better our breed, we now have purchased this 'phenomenal boy' for our future stallion."

The ultimate goal of Appaloosa breeders has always been to produce the one horse that will influence the breed like no other. Many breeders—both past and present—have accomplished that dream through horses that out-produce and out-perform their predecessors. Because of this, the Appaloosa horse continues to evolve, bringing to the forefront the most outstanding color and athleticism ever. Indeed, the Appaloosa is the horse to watch and see what surprises it holds for the future.

Top: Proud Reflection gets a smile from a mare.
Bottom: Showing off. Proud Reflection, Old River Ranch, Harvard, Idaho, owned by Tom and Joanne O'Brien.
Photos by Jason Abbott.

Top and *bottom*: Shaking off the dust. Proud Reflection, Old River Ranch, Harvard, Idaho, owned by Tom and Joanne O'Brien. Photos by Jason Abbott.

BABIES, BABIES

Appaloosa Foals

Businesses that raise Appaloosas chose the breed for good reasons. They love the surprise of color, they love the Appaloosa's temperament, and they love the fun of watching the miracles of life occur each year—to name a few. Breeding Appaloosas can be a lucrative venture, but there is so much more quality and richness to it than mere business transactions. The excitement, the relationships, the risk—all make breeding and raising Appaloosa foals an adventure.

Finding the right combination of bloodlines to ensure good conformation, a good mind, and that extra bonus—spots—is an ongoing process for some Appaloosa

Kaden Abbott at Gramps Appaloosas, Princeton, Idaho. Photo by Jason Abbott.

Easter Foal

It was Easter morning, 1966. As we rounded the bend of the gravel road on our way home from church and saw our house in the distance, I immediately searched the pasture for my Appaloosa mare. She was heavy in foal. I was 10 years old, and I couldn't wait to see her baby. My maternal instincts were incredibly strong for my age. I had tried on several occasions to save baby birds that had fallen from their nests, and when they always died, I cried as if I'd lost my best friend. I'd spend hours in the barn watching the new calves and always loved it when we could bring the mother pig's runt of the litter into the house for bottle-feeding.   *There she was in the pasture, grazing as usual. From a distance, it looked like our big black German Shepherd dog was nearby, watching her. Strange, I thought, but dismissed it right away. My grandparents were there for Easter dinner, and as we drove up the driveway, they were waiting for us beside the wood fence, waving and smiling. I loved it when they visited. After our hugs, I tore into the house to change my clothes and run down to the pasture to check on the mare.*   *When I came down the stairs from my room in my jeans and tee shirt, my mother said, "Your horse had her baby." I couldn't believe it! I started to run out the door, but she stopped me. "Don't," she said. "Let dad and grandpa check on it first." It seemed like an eternity before they came back up to the house.*   *"It's a filly," they said. That wasn't the dog in the pasture, it was the foal, they told me.*   *I ran to the pasture to meet my very first foal. I'll never forget how small she seemed as she stood beside her blue roan, spotted mother. A dark bay with two white socks at birth, she later developed a sprinkling of white spots on her rump. For*

Newborn foal near Kooskia, Idaho. Photo by Kevin Pullen.

months after she was born, whenever mom or dad wanted to find me, they knew just where I'd be. Right there, sleeping beside her in the field, teaching her to lead, mauling her with affection—or just sitting in the pasture watching her. She required a lot of care and attention, but she always gave back so much more. She was one of my partners in life that taught me lessons in a way that no one else could, like gentle persistence, patience, and strength. She and her mother embodied that Appaloosa spirit, capable of partnering with a little girl in an astounding, life-changing way. I will always be grateful.

Top and *bottom*: Sheldak Ranch, Sheldon, North Dakota. Photos by owner Kim Utke.

Laci, Taci, and Briar Welch, TW Show Horses, Marysville, Ohio. Photo by Kim Welch.

breeders. Studying pedigrees and envisioning that "perfect" Appaloosa coat pattern is the starting point when searching for stallions and mares that will match up to produce the most desirable foals. Many find one stallion that consistently produces champion foals, while others search for years to find the right one. It's a process and a quest that Appaloosa breeders wouldn't give up.

What foals come to mean to many people makes it a wonder that they are ever sold, which is why finding good homes is so paramount to breeders and why most breeders follow the success of the foals they've bred with pride and a continued sense of ownership.

Tom and Kim Welch, who own TW Show Horses in Marysville, Ohio, stand the stallion Doncha Wanna Moon Me at their ranch. Kim says, "What's special about our stallion is his heritage and the legacy left by his sire Moon Me. He also has a unique personality. There's just something about him that you have to know to experience. As Brian Raggio once said about Doncha Wanna Moon Me's sire, 'You just

Palisades
Appaloosas,
Lancaster,
Kentucky.
Photo by
owner
Lisa Estridge.

Sheldak Ranch, Sheldon, North Dakota.
Photos by owner Kim Utke.

Sheldak Ranch, Sheldon, North Dakota.
Photos by owner Kim Utke.

don't breed horses like him everyday.' But then there's his color and coat pattern, which is phenomenal."

"We are all about the Appaloosas," Kim says. "They also have great dispositions and versatility. We love the excitement of carefully choosing mares to cross with stallions until that perfect, champion offspring is created. But the most exciting part of breeding Appaloosas for our family is foaling season, when each and every new life is a surprise from the start. What is produced is never the same as the picture you have painted in your mind." They also love the hands-on experience that their kids, Laci, Taci, and Briar, have and that they are able to witness the actual birth of the foals. "Our children have been raised around the horses and enjoy the life that we have chosen for them," Kim says.

Tom and Kim were both brought up around horses. "Our business of promoting the Appaloosa breed is a way of life for us," says Kim. Although it requires a lot of dedication, hard work, commitment, and responsibility, they have found that if you give your all, the rewards of breeding Appaloosas are priceless.

Photo by Monika Hannawacker, Schönaúak, Germany

The Legendary Appaloosa

Parturition

The complex process of breeding and birthing is as much a perfect scientific chain of events as it is a miraculous event to witness. Nancy Braskin shares her story of the excitement and preparation of her first foal's birth. ◆ I bred my mare and waited eleven long months for the arrival of the foal. To prepare me for the birth, I talked to a few experts and picked up a few books to get ready for the big event. ◆ "Parturition is a complex cascade of physiologic events," reproductive physiologist Phil Senger tells me. "The fetus actually initiates the onset of labor by releasing a hormone that begins the process." ◆ "There are three stages of labor for a mare," the book titled Blessed Are the Brood Mares said. The first stage is internal and nearly

Sheldak Ranch, Sheldon, North Dakota. Photo by owner Kim Utke.

Photo by Ursula Lise, The Netherlands.

Sheldak Ranch, Sheldon, North Dakota.
Photo by owner Kim Utke.

invisible unless you're watching closely. You might notice that the mare's sides have suddenly become flatter, indicating that the foal has dropped into the birth canal. "Ready for delivery and pushed up into the birth canal with intact placental tissue through dilated cervix," *I continued to read. You might also see restlessness, sweating, digging, tail switching or quietly eating.* She quietly eats and switches her tail all the time, *I thought.* I hope I can tell the difference. ◆

I also learned that the heart rate increases and the body temperature decreases. "It is *most important that this stage not be missed because once labor (the*

Invied, owned by Weibe and Ursula Lise. Photo by Ursula Lise, The Netherlands.

Photo by owner Ursula Lise, The Netherlands.

second stage) has commenced, there is no provision for delay as exists in other species." *Internally, the uterine walls are changing shape and contracting, moving the 11-month fetus from one horn of the uterus to the central location. "At this time the foal is ideally presented in a dorsosacral position; that is, the spinal axis of the foal is in a parallel plane with the spinal axis of the dam, with both forelegs preceding the head."* Okay, I need to see the feet first. *The first stage of labor culminates with a sudden gush of water and the appearance of a grayish-white sac with a foot inside. This stage of labor usually lasts one to four hours.* ◆ *"The foal may be compared with an astronaut or a deep-sea diver," the book continued. In other words, as long as all its support systems remain intact during delivery, the baby can continue to survive in its own sac. The second stage of labor has now begun with the breaking of the placental membranes. Once this stage has begun, "time is precious and very short—strict, alert watchfulness is essential. Delivery will progress relentlessly until completed."* ◆ *I learned that the foal is*

Sheldak Ranch, Sheldon, North Dakota. Photo by owner Kim Utke.

Palisades Appaloosas, Lancaster, Kentucky. Photo by owner Lisa Estridge.

actually inside two sacs. One has just ruptured, but the other still encases the foal until delivery. The first rupturing has lubricated the mare's reproductive tract for an easier delivery. Magnificent. ◆ *Some mares remain standing, and some lie down during delivery. "If it is clear that the mare intends to foal standing, then help is required. One person should stand at the mare's head and another should catch the foal to prevent it from dropping to the ground and prematurely rupturing the cord or possibly sustaining injury to its head, neck, or spine."* Oh my. ◆ *"If the sac is not visible after several contractions, the attendant should rapidly scrub hands and arms, cup the fingers, enter the vulvar lips and locate the lodged foot of the foal. Place the palm over the sharp little foot*

to shield it from the roof of the vagina. The mare's reproductive future may be preserved by this simple, essential fact," I read. If the sac does not appear for any other reason, *"summon help immediately."* Now I'm taking notes, writing down vet's phone number, sister's phone number, best friend's phone number. ◆ *But—given the chance that the delivery is "normal," the attendant should just stand back and watch the miracle of life happen. But when the front feet and legs are well in sight, the second membrane can be opened (with scissors!) and turned back from the foal, if you really feel the need, the book says. Stage two of labor lasts 12 to 30 minutes.* ◆ *"Do not hurry the mare's delivery," the book cautioned. Let nature take its course, but remember, "There is no reason for alarm at the sight of a blue tongue extending from the foal's mouth." Apparently, the foal begins breathing once its hind feet are delivered, and is stimulated by reflex. But—just in case the foal does not breathe, "every effort should be made to clear the nasal passages of fluids." This can be done with a small rubber bulb. Once the foal is completely delivered, you can rub his entire body with the towels you have ready* (I quickly add two more items to my list: rubber bulb and towels), *because that stimulates circulation and creates warmth. It can also reduce some initial stress for the foal.* ◆ *It is of utmost importance to prevent premature rupture of the umbilical cord. Even though the foal is on the ground and dried off, the umbilical cord is still supporting the foal because there is about a pint of oxygenated blood that passes from the maternal placenta into the foal's circulatory system.* Wow. *The foal will eventually kick away from the mare and rupture the cord naturally. The umbilical cord should never be severed other than by natural means,* I continued to read, feeling slightly anxious. ◆ *"Stage three of labor involves expulsion of the placental membranes, about one hour after delivery, and the beginning of a healing process for the mare, which takes around 30 days. Ovarian activity resumes in only 5-12 days.* ◆ *The placenta should be examined closely to make sure that it is all there to be sure that no fragments are retained by the mare that might cause infection,"* the book tells me, displaying photos of the placenta to help me identify all the parts. *"The postpartum pain that the dam suffers looks similar to colic: rolling, kicking, tail switching, straining, sweating."* If all goes well, the mare can be re-bred during her foal heat in about three weeks. And the process starts all over again. ◆ Amazing!

The Surprise

"My Appaloosas are very special to me," says Kathy Speck of Zephyrhills, Florida. "My first Appaloosa, Sparkel And Shine, or Shania, is a palomino mare with a white blanket and spots, and was purchased in 2003. She and I have a very special bond, and I wouldn't and couldn't sell this horse for a million dollars. I took Shania home and wanted to get started with her immediately.

"As a few weeks passed, I noticed she wasn't driving great from her back end; she had slow gaits, just not deep in the back. I figured something was up. She was sore for some reason. I took her to the vet to check her out and also make sure that she was breeding sound, since I had already purchased a breeding for her with Mr. Cool Hand Luke, owned by Frank Larrabee. The vet started the exam and soon his face turned red, he was laughing so hard. 'How old is your mare and has she ever been bred?' Shania was four years old and a maiden mare at the time—I thought! The vet, Dr. Sam Thomas, said that she was in heavy foal and that is why she wasn't driving!

"April rolled around and Shania was waxed up and I was a nervous wreck. I had every name and number of anyone that could help me out on foaling night listed on an

Palisades Appaloosas, Lancaster, Kentucky. Photo by owner Lisa Estridge.

Sheldak Ranch,
Sheldon, North Dakota.
Photo by owner Kim Utke.

Gramps Appaloosas, Princeton, Idaho. Photo by Jessica Wright.

Sheldak Ranch, Sheldon, North Dakota. Photo by owner Kim Utke.

8- by 10-inch card. I also had my foal kit and stall bedded with straw, ready since January. On April 19, 2004, at 9 p.m. Shania's water broke. She was having some difficulty, so I called a family friend that raises Belgians. Luckily he was close by. Shania had a pinched nerve after foaling, so I had called the vet for some assistance. In the meantime, my dad had called the rest of my immediate family, and we all had a mini-party.

"Shania's new foal, which I named Bianca, was finally here. She was so cute and ornery! She is gray with a white blanket and now towers over Shania and is a very sweet-tempered filly."

Kathy bred Shania on her foal heat to Mr. Cool Hand Luke. The year rolled around fast and Shania showed no signs of foaling. Kathy checked on her every morning before work and every night, and finally got a call at work saying that she had a buckskin colt with spots on his hips. "I about flipped out—all of my foaling kits, cameras, and videos were of no use. Shania foaled around noon and the colt was here. Diesel, or Heza Lukey Charm, is just that—a charming little man. He floats on air and has a type of finesse to him.

"He is so patient with me fussing with him, and I can't wait to start showing him. I consider it pretty much an honor to say that I own Appaloosas," Kathy says.

Sheldak Ranch, Sheldon, North Dakota. Photo by owner Kim Utke.

A Note to My Foal

Early this morning I saw you for the first time far at the bottom of the field where the fence borders the birch trees, beneath the cool shade. All of my reading and anxiety to prepare for your birth had been useless, because you arrived without me even knowing—three full weeks early. We had waited forever for you it seemed, though, watching your mother's belly grow each week, stretched taut with your weight and length. In the beginning my husband had said, "I don't think she's pregnant." But I told him I was sure I saw a small bulge right there, beside her flank. I inspected it each night at first, and before long we were both convinced that she really was in foal. ◆ As you grew, I scratched your mother's underside each evening, remembering how my own skin itched with the tightness of a growing

Sheldak Ranch, Sheldon, North Dakota. Photo by owner Kim Utke.

Sheldak Ranch, Sheldon, North Dakota. Photo by owner Kim Utke.

baby. "I wonder if she understands what's happening to her," I asked my husband several times. "I wonder how they know what to do." "It's instinct," he always answered. But still, I wanted to be there when you were born, just in case it wasn't. ◆ When I saw you, right away I ran to the bottom of the field to feel your wet baby hair and to touch your small pink and gray hooves; your tiny, white muzzle. I laughed when I saw the perfect pink square on the end of it. You were afraid of me at first, but slowly reached out to say hello. I inspected every inch of you, just to make sure you were complete, all the time praising your mother for a job well done. You were her first—a miracle, as every new life is. You wobbled to your feet and tested your strength and gravity as I sat in the trampled grass nearby wondering at your fresh perspective on the world. Before I knew it, half the day was gone and I was still watching you. ◆ Through your eyes, I've looked at life differently. We spoke to you, as much as possible, using your own language, always praising and encouraging any attempt by you to do what we asked. Your mother watched us closely, but never interfered. Such a

Sheldak Ranch, Sheldon, North Dakota. Photo by owner Kim Utke.

good mare, such a wise mother. ◆ *Each day we asked you for some small gift. "If I push gently on you here, will you move away from me?" "Can I take this halter and put it over your nose, just for a second?" As soon as you said "yes," we asked no more, but showered you with hugs and pats, then asked for a little more the next day. You loved that. Before long, you became so sensitive, so wise, so trusting. Your breeding assured us that you would be an athlete, but your mother gave you something more: her gentle temperament and her incredible sensibility. Since you came into our lives, we have learned so much about our world and yours. You are a part of what completes our lives.*

Palisades Appaloosas, Lancaster, Kentucky. Photo by owner Lisa Estridge.

Top and *bottom*: Sheldak Ranch, Sheldon, North Dakota. Photos by owner Kim Utke.

Kendall Samford and Twice the Wrangler. Photo by Jan Bard.

MY FINEST FRIEND

Companionship

I use to lay in bed and dream that I would wake up and find an Appaloosa in our barn for me.

—SHARLENE ADAMS

Appaloosas make the best kids' companions. Not only are they gentle and intelligent, they own a unique sensibility that enables them to inherently understand that kids are valuable cargo. Just put a small child on the back of an Appaloosa and you'll see the horse drop his head and stand quietly. Appaloosas are so gentle and trustworthy that they are often used in therapeutic riding programs for kids and adults with disabilities.

Appaloosas have been known to help kids—and adults—through the toughest times and teach them valuable life lessons. Many horses might be considered a surrogate parent that gently guides a person through life. Take Jessica Stemmler and her Appaloosa Mighty Goer Blaze, for example.

"With Blaze," Jessica says, "I learned who I am in this world, and what I stand for. He has shaped who I was into who I am and who I plan on being."

Like many adolescents, when Jessica was in middle school, she was rebellious, depressed, and looking for purpose in life. But then she went to a week of horse camp, and her life changed forever. She says that the horses she met at camp were "God reaching out to me on Earth."

A year later Jessica started taking riding lessons, and the following year she received Blaze as a birthday present.

"With him I found a horse I could pour my heart out to. A horse I could call my own and never worry about leaving. A horse whose heart I could steal just as he stole mine. I could feel him telling me, 'You need to be here because I need you.' I had found my passion, my reason for living, in his spirit."

Kaden Abbott, Gramps Appaloosas, Princeton, Idaho. Photo by Jessica Wright.

Monika Hannawacker and Dear Little Cisco. Photo by Manuela Steininger, Germany.

Sydney Bard of Bar-D Ranch, Maple Valley, Washington. Photo by Jan Bard.

Kaden Abbott, Gramps Appaloosas, Princeton, Idaho. Photo by Jason Abbott.

Laura Abbott, Gramps Appaloosas, Princeton, Idaho. Photo by Jason Abbott.

Hannah Jo Michalak on I Dream of Sadie, Old River Ranch, Harvard, Idaho. Photo by Kevin Pullen.

Maggie Swick, 2006 Chief Joseph Trail Ride. Photo by Kevin Pullen.

Winter on the ranch. Dave Utke, Sheldak Ranch, Sheldon, North Dakota. Photo by owner Kim Utke.

That was the beginning of a new life for Jessica, filled with challenges and lessons, but most of all enhanced by a relationship that still endures. Blaze has not only taught her passion, but the ability to make strong decisions and the ability to feel—which is her favorite lesson of all.

"Blaze taught me to sense nature and other people's feelings and react to them, just as he reacts to me when I'm sad or mad or excited. To be able to sense things opens a whole world up to you."

Blaze turned Jessica's life around and set her on a pathway that she never dreamed possible. "This one Appaloosa is the only horse I believe could have done this all for me," she says. "He was a gift in more ways than one. I have been granted strength and confidence and skill. I have been changed, and my life will forever be one with horses."

Jessica's story is universal. Countless people can attest to the fact that their relationship with a special horse carried them through some of their most difficult years and set them on a path towards healing, success, and fulfillment.

Apart from filling emotional needs, Appaloosas serve other equally important functions in life. Caring for horses and riding them teaches responsibility, caretaking, hard work, and structure. For those who show, the horse teaches what it's like to compete with and support others. It creates bonds in many ways—not just with the horse, but also with other horse people.

Following are stories contributed by Appaloosa lovers. Their stories attest to the powerful, rich relationship that they enjoy with their beloved horses and the special bond that transcends time and space.

Snoqualmie

By Lisa Wysocky, Nashville, Tennessee

I was a horse-crazy kid from the time I was 2 until...well, until now. The summer I turned 12, I got an Appaloosa mare and named her Snoqualmie, after an area in western Washington near where Appaloosas became known. She became my best friend.

I lived in Minnesota, and during the summers of my early teen years, friends and I would play polo or cowboys and Indians. We'd take our horses down to the lake and use them as diving boards. Long trail rides through meandering woods were a regular occurrence. In the winter, I'd hook Snoqualmie to a toboggan and she'd pull me down snow-covered farm roads.

As I grew older, Snoqualmie became my 4-H project, my youth horse at local saddle club shows, and then my game horse. When I was saddle club queen, she was my grand entry horse. She loved pole weaving and loved to jump. Her smooth gaits ensured that we were tough competition on a state level in the Egg and Spoon race.

Rachel Pozzi and Impressive Ms Go Go, 2006 Youth World Appaloosa Show. Photo by Diane Rice.

When I was in high school, weather permitting, I'd clamber aboard Snoqualmie while she was grazing in the pasture and lie backwards, facing her tail, as I struggled with homework.

When I took a job as a trail guide at a local dude ranch, Snoqualmie became my guide horse, and when I began giving riding lessons, she was my lesson horse. I took Snoqualmie to college with me, then to a training job in Ohio and then to Washington State. She became my pony horse when I was exercising yearlings, the horse I rode to check fences, and the one I chose to ride when I just wanted to ride.

When I started my own stable, she was my main lesson horse, and she was amazing. When a young child was riding, she'd walk so slowly and carefully you'd

Photo by Jason Abbott.

Riders on the Chief Joseph Trail Ride. Photo by Kristen Reiter.

have thought she was walking on eggshells. When the rider became more secure, she refused to do anything unless she was asked firmly and correctly. An advanced rider could excel on her in anything from barrel racing to dressage. When I took a terrible fall that damaged my knee and ultimately ended my career as a trainer of Appaloosa horses, she was the horse I first got back up on. She was the horse that delivered me from the fear of falling again.

Snoqualmie was very intelligent and had a wonderful sense of humor. Another trainer and I once watched as she let herself out of a locked box stall, opened the stall doors of four other horses, then went back into her own stall. She slammed the sliding door shut with her nose before she turned to watch all the fun.

Snoqualmie followed me south, and in her later years became my son's horse. When he was 5, they'd canter together across the pasture, bareback, no bridle, her mane flying and he laughing with glee. They'd play pirates with our big black dog, Dexter, Snoqualmie alternately playing the parts of racehorse, Indian fort, ship, or flying saucer, wearing the costumes that went along with the role.

When she was in her late twenties, Snoqualmie developed a thyroid deficiency, then foundered in a rear leg. In her 30th year, she was felled by a stroke. She died just before Christmas in 1992 and is buried on a farm outside of Nashville. It has become a tradition for my son and me to visit her each Thanksgiving Day.

For 23 years Snoqualmie was my friend, my companion, my sister. I knew when I called her that she wasn't going to come until she dipped her head once and tilted her nose to the right. She knew during a riding lesson if I took two steps back and crossed my arms, I was going to ask the student to trot her. From her I learned the important things in life: friendship, determination, trust, and responsibility. After Snoqualmie's passing, I searched for a way to let people know how much she, and other horses, meant to me. As my way of thanking Snoqualmie for sharing her life with me, I named my public relations firm, White Horse Enterprises, after her, and I wrote a book about country music stars and their horses called *The Power of Horses*, in which Snoqualmie was featured.

Recently, I began training horses for therapeutic riding programs, and I share my stories of Snoqualmie with disabled children. So even now, more than a decade after her death, Snoqualmie brightens not only my day, but the day of many children who never knew her.

Big Time Grin

By Ina Ziegler, Olympia, Washington

Our interest in Appaloosas began when a friend recommended my daughter, Christa, who was 8 years old at the time, to an Appaloosa breeder and trainer. Her former mount, an energetic Arab mare, was handed down to me, since I wanted to begin trail riding. It soon became evident that trail riding was not something this mare liked very much, but I couldn't buy another horse at the time. Christa continued her training on the beautiful and personality-filled Appaloosa gelding we'd purchased for her.

Sometimes, when I returned home from trail rides, my father would be waiting there, having come for a visit. He always had a huge grin on his face and loved seeing me out enjoying my horse time, especially since I came to it fairly late in my life. I always looked forward to seeing him and his big smile.

Eventually my dad became ill with pancreatic cancer—a very aggressive and quickly debilitating disease. He wanted to see Christa and I continue with our horse activities, so he helped me buy a new trailer. Although he was too ill to come out

Sara E. Michalak on Spotted Image "Abby," Old River Ranch, Harvard, Idaho. Photo by Kevin Pullen.

and tour the trailer, he watched out his window as I opened doors and windows and pointed out its features from afar.

All too soon, cancer took Dad's life. My family mourned, celebrated his life with friends and family, and took care of all that needed doing, including a trip to his favorite place in eastern Washington to distribute his ashes. Soon after that trip, I donated my Arab mare as a therapeutic horse, which left me without a mount and

Monika Hannawacker and Cisco at Biburg, Germany. Photo by Manuela Steininger.

in the market for a trail horse. I bought a 4-year-old Appaloosa from Christa's trainer. Although he had no trail experience and was young, he was wonderful from the get go. He's become very special to me.

When it came time to register my new Appaloosa, I found out that he was by Big Time Zippo and out of Impish Grin, and my thoughts went to my dad and that big smile he always had waiting for me at the end of the drive. With all the fun memories my Appaloosa had already given me, I couldn't think of a more fitting name to honor my dad's memory than to name my new horse "Gotta Big Time Grin."

Thanks Dad—I love you!

Michelle Bobbitt, 2006 Chief Joseph Trail Ride. Photo by Kevin Pullen.

Snowflake

BY CHERYL DUDLEY, MOSCOW, IDAHO

My husband and I leaned against the wood rail fence one evening watching our mare with her newborn foal. We could see the dark silhouette of the bay colt, white snip glowing in the moonlight, as he ran circles around his mom, only to dart off into the darkness of the field. Fancy, my mare, pranced around anxiously, chasing her new son here and there and trying to nudge him to stay close to her. But he wouldn't have it. He finally ran through and behind the gate near us,

Dear Little Cisco and Tobys Spot Carlito. Photo by owner Monika Hannawacker, Germany.

Dustin Steedman, Sheldak Ranch, Sheldon, North Dakota. Photo by owner Kim Utke.

2006 Chief Joseph Trail riders. Photo by Kevin Pullen.

where his fretting mother immediately blocked him from running off. The two stood quietly for a few moments behind the open gate while she nickered softly to him, then the mare slowly guided the foal into the barn stall where she could keep a closer eye on him.

Horses communicate with each other with body language, and watching Fancy with her baby brought home to me the power of their silent communication and the complex balance between allowing freedom while protecting from harm.

But more than anything, the mare and foal made me think of my relationship with my dad. Because he rarely spoke to me, I learned to read him and interpret his gestures and movements, trying hard to extract his acceptance of me through his smallest expressions. And it was appropriate for me to think of him at that moment, since it was because of him that I loved horses.

Jessica Gross, Chief Joseph Trail Ride. Photo by Kevin Pullen.

Yearling Appaloosa eye. Photo by Kevin Pullen.

When I was small, my dad seemed to know that unless my energy was harnessed, I could end up in trouble. Although we had owned horses since I was young, we went through a period of time after I went into the third grade without horses because my dad became unemployed, which meant moving around until he found a job.

By the time we settled down in Troy, Idaho, we were horseless, and I was 9 years old. We lived on 35 acres of rolling Palouse hills and forests equipped with barns and small sheds—but we were too poor to buy horses. Eventually my parents, concerned that my sisters and I were too bored, surprised us with a donkey. "Jack" was just as stubborn as the stories of donkeys depict, and although I loved him, he still fell short of the speed and freedom I longed for in a horse.

One day my dad told me to get in the car, that we were going someplace, but he couldn't tell me where. We drove in silence to a small horse farm about three miles down the road. Without a word, we got out of the car. I watched Dad's face closely to see if I could read what was going on.

"See that Appaloosa over there?" Dad said.

I looked over to the round pen that held a beautiful Appaloosa horse with a white mane and tail.

"Yes, I see it," I said to my dad.

"She's yours," he said.

I felt like someone had just crowned me princess of the universe. I wasn't sure that I had heard him correctly.

"She's really mine?" I said.

"She's yours," my dad chuckled. "And she's going to have a foal."

As I stood on the fence watching my new horse, I couldn't find the words to thank my father. I hoped that he understood my inability to express how I felt. Yet, looking back, I wish that I had said more. I wish that I had thrown my arms around him and thanked him a zillion times. But that would have been unlike us. We communicated in more subtle ways.

That was the beginning of an amazing era in my life. Every day I woke up, bridled Snowflake, and took off. Preferring to ride bareback, I ran through the fields and meadows, one with my horse in a way that I never dreamed possible. The sights that I galloped upon, at times, were surreal. A doe with twin fawns grazing in a meadow; a group of porcupines feasting on a field of peas; a heard of elk nibbling the new spring wheat; the sound of the breeze through tall tamaracks; standing beneath a pine canopy waiting for a spring rainfall to pass. These memories represent a most vital part of my childhood, planting a yearning in me that would never again be satisfied without a horse, a trail, and the woods.

The emotions that overwhelmed me the following Easter morning that Snowflake's foal was born were nearly as powerful as the mornings, many years later, when my own sons were born. I rode Snowflake bareback the day before she delivered the little bay filly that I called Heidi. I had an immense sense of ownership over Heidi—almost as if Snowflake and I together had created this wonderful, miniature creature. Before long I had a halter on her, then a saddle. I was riding her when she was barely 2 years old. Soon she developed a small sprinkling of spots on her rump, while her mother became whiter each year.

For years my Appaloosa horses were my life, filling the void in my heart. I could talk to Snowflake about anything and she always listened attentively and never condemned me for how I felt. We co-existed in a way, above a quilted world with her mane against my face, her breath against my cupped palm. The world we created together wasn't one that could be touched, but only sensed upon the wind or in her deep blue eyes. Back then I didn't know how to describe my horse and I. I only knew that I longed to be with her always—that her spirit had somehow merged with mine and we were as one. Even now, as I write this, I feel her presence.

High school, boys, and finally marriage took me away from horses for nearly 20 years. Snowflake was sold to a man down the road who used her as a broodmare. She produced many spotted foals, and when I visited home after I married, I took my sons by her pasture to show them how she still raised her head when I whistled. I found out, years later, that Snowflake lived to be nearly 32 years old.

My husband knew my horse story, and many years after Snowflake and my dad were gone, bought me this mare named Fancy, and had her bred. Throughout her pregnancy, my mind drifted back many times to Snowflake and the little Easter foal named Heidi, and inevitably I think of my dad and his incredible gift to me. My dad placed me in the care of a horse, knowing that she'd understand and guide me through my most formidable years.

Laura Abbott, Gramps Appaloosas, Princeton, Idaho. Photo by Jason Abbott.

What defines a horse person? If you write horse stories for English class, do coat color genetics for Biology, read horse magazines in your spare time, and spend nearly every hour of your free time at the barn, then you are a horse person.

—Jessica Stemmler

As with any venture, breeding foals does include risk. This is an element of what Lisa Estridge, of Lancaster, Kentucky, shares when she talks about one of her favorite and most memorable foals, Palisades Morning Glory. This foal made a lasting impact on Lisa's life and on many others who have read her story.

Palisades Morning Glory

By Lisa Estridge, Lancaster, Kentucky

June 30

Glory had been born normal, but at two weeks, I noticed she couldn't keep up with her dam. We brought her to an equine hospital when she was five weeks old. The doc said she most likely had an abscess on her spine. Glory stayed at the hospital for 10 days. She was given megadoses of antibiotics and steroids. In just two days on the intravenous anti-inflammatory medicines, Glory could get up on her own. She was wobbly and would last only an hour or so, but she could nurse and move around the stall before going down again.

Glory gained strength, but when we removed the medications, she could no longer get up. We replaced her medicines with weaker medicines and continued two kinds of antibiotics. By day 10, it was time to take her home and continue her nursing care on the farm.

Glory has been home for three weeks and she is now 10 weeks old. She has grown and filled out, despite her illness. Her personality is wonderful. She is so loving and tolerant. She is now out in the pasture by day with Peaches, her dam, and tries to trot and canter in her wobbly fashion. She even tries a few bucks, although not much is happening on the hind end! Just this week, she has been staying on her feet for 12 to 14 hours, from morning to lights out in the barn. The bad news is that she still cannot get up on her own most of the time. I have to lift her at ll p.m, 3 a.m., and 7 a.m. The nights are long and sleep is short.

July 17

Glory no longer likes me to help her up. If I go into her stall and suggest it, she looks at me as if to say "No thanks, I'm comfy!" So I take Peaches and walk out of the stall. After a minute or two of struggle, Glory is up and coming after us, wagging her head and saying WAIT FOR ME!!! I have not lifted her up for two days.

In the pasture, she still stumbles easily and has an unsteady gait on the hind end, but she trots frequently and seems to enjoy her time out nibbling, scratching on the fence, and evading flies. They stay out a good 6 or 8 hours a day now. On July the 9th, my birthday, Glory gave me a gift. I saw her stumble and fall in the pasture...and get up by herself without much trouble. What a lovely birthday present for me...hope!

I don't know just how far Glory can or will recover, but I want to say I am getting dangerously hopeful about the possibility of a long life for this special filly.

July 26

July is almost over and I have been caring for Glory for two months. Progress is slow. She is holding her own and making tiny strides forward. The last two nights, Glory has gotten up on her own. I saw her on my monitor and did not have to leave my bed.

A week from now Glory will no longer be on antibiotics. This will be a moment of truth. If the infection returns, I think we will be defeated. At nine weeks, we feel that the infection should be gone, and any impairment we see now is nerve damage that will have to be overcome by physical therapy and time. If Glory can stay stable off medicines, I am willing to give her a long, long time to recover from the damage done to her nervous system and all the help she needs. This will be sink or swim for Glory. We are so hoping she can swim!

August 9

Glory has been off her antibiotics one week. So far I see no decline. In fact, I have seen some improvement in her occasional attempts to canter. Today she was in a heavy downpour. She got very frisky and tried a few bucks and runs. She slipped on the mud and wet grass and fell right on her bottom, but got up quickly despite very slippery footing. We are still optimistic, but not counting any chickens until more time passes for Glory.

August 22

Glory has been off antibiotics for 18 days. For two weeks she continued to get up on her own at night and enjoy the pasture by day with her mom. One morning, I tried turning the two out with the herd, and Glory was so excited she put on a show for us. She tried some running sidekicks and bucking, and it looked like she was doing deep knee bends and hops or having some sort of aerial seizure.

August 26

Just when I was feeling very optimistic, I noticed Glory's gait become more uneven. For the last two days, I have seen a decline...not a huge one, but it's there. I have dreaded the thought that once off antibiotics, the abscess could begin to grow again and press upon her spine.

I had a long talk with Glory tonight while massaging her back and legs. I told her I have done all I can do and the rest is up to her. We are still hoping for the best, but realize that we are observers at this point. Glory's recovery is not in our hands.

August 30

Good news today. I am thrilled to say that Glory has a sore front foot, not pressure on her spine. I found a horizontal crack below her heel and managed to clean the feet last night while she was resting. She has been going out to pasture and acting pretty spunky despite a small head bob on that front right.

Glory is four months old and never been led, so today we had a leading lesson. Was she annoyed with me! What on earth is this rope on me! Don't I get to be a princess and walk wherever and whenever I want?

I led Glory to the pasture and she was all over the place, yanking and trotting and bucking on the lead line. We were just howling at this performance as I was dancing everywhere trying to give to the lead line just enough not to cause her a

Dustin Steedman, Sheldak Ranch, Sheldon, North Dakota. Photo by owner Kim Utke.

wreck. When I set her free, she pranced and bucked, and I saw an honest to good-ness canter uphill. Downhill, I saw her being extremely careful. She fell over on her back on that same hill one morning at turnout because the ground was wet. I think she remembered. Did I expect anything less than a smart Glory?

September 6

Glory has had a relapse.

Saturday night I noticed her having some difficulty rising, and by Sunday evening, I saw Glory down in the field and not able to get up. I can lift her, and she can stand and walk, but she has taken a huge decline.

I can see in her eyes that she is upset that I have to lift her again.

September 15

I have a heavy heart and mind today. Glory is very ill. She seems to have pain and does not want to rise or walk any more than she has to. No fever, nothing to see, ex-cept her hind end is growing weaker and more spastic. She is still barely moving.

I have taken in a blood sample to try and understand more about what is killing this sweet young horse. Whatever it is, it's about killing me too. She came so far toward normal and now is back to where we began.

September 18

Glory's blood tests were somewhat unexpected. She had several values that were very low.

I am not ready to let her go yet. Maybe there is one more miracle for this strong filly.

September 24

In a big foaling stall full of hay, I helped Glory into the world. I helped her to stand and nurse. At five weeks old, when she lost the use of her legs, I again helped her to stand and nurse through the day and night. Together we journeyed through illness to health, and Glory cantered and played with her mother and enjoyed the summer.

She began to lose her ability to get up and her joints became sore and upright. We hoped for simple problems with simple solutions and treated her pain, but last night a vicious fever erupted. When I saw the thermometer at 104.8, I cooled her in water and took her temperature again. It was 105.

In that moment I knew that my time with Glory was almost over.

This morning I helped Glory to rest. I had cooled her fever, but I knew in my heart that further treatment would not likely lead to long-term recovery. Infection that invades at birth so often hides and resurfaces again and again. Glory was fat and beautiful this morning, and I would not let her decline and become debilitated with infection and pain. I told the vet to stay outside and I sneaked an injection of sedative into Glory's neck while she enjoyed some grain. She looked at me as if I were a pest and shook her neck. In about 10 minutes she was so sleepy that the vet was able to quietly give her the lethal injection that ended her life.

She took a part of me with her. I will miss her so. I have never loved an animal as much.

I am still here in this field, waiting to see your spotted coat, your bucks and pranks, your love for life. I cannot let go of my memories of you.

—CAD

Savannah Buttice, 2006 Chief Joseph Trail Ride. Photo by Kevin Pullen.

TACK UP FOR THE TRAIL

"All good things are wild and free."
—HENRY DAVID THOREAU, *WALKING* (1862)

I went to the woods because I wished to live deliberately, to front only the essential facts of life, and see if I could not learn what it had to teach, and not, when I came to die, discover that I had not lived.

—HENRY DAVID THOREAU, *WALDEN* (1854)

Trail riding is one of the most pure recreational activities that remain in our fast-paced world. Becoming one with nature on an Appaloosa horse has the potential to stroke the soul and reach deep into our innate sense of spirituality, reconnecting us with life's most important and fundamental meanings.

George Hatley (left) on Toby II, and Clyde Spenser on Freckled Gal near Helmer, Idaho, 1950.
Photo courtesy of Rita Koontz.

2006 Chief Joseph Trail Ride. Photo by Kristin Reiter.

Riding a high mountain range. Photo by Jan Bard.

Mike and Barbara Croy, 2006 Chief Joseph Trail Ride. Photo by Kristen Reiter.

Spending time in nature reminds us that we, too, are part of an immense world that consists of vast blue skies, cold mountain lakes, towering tamaracks—and our beloved Appaloosa horses.

Given the physical challenges and required athleticism of trail riding, it makes sense that the Appaloosa horse is the choice breed for the sport. Because Appaloosas were bred by the Indians for sure-footedness on the trail and a placid demeanor, many trail riders choose them, not just for athleticism, but also for intelligence,

Linze Bard riding a Montana trail. Photo by Jan Bard.

bombproof temperaments, and smooth gaits. The bottom line is that Appaloosas can be trusted on the trail.

Appaloosa owners will attest to the fact that this breed is particularly hardy on steep mountain trails where endurance and agility are important. While other breeds might tire or break down in tough terrain, the Appaloosa maintains amazing stamina. Foundation-bred Appaloosas boast solid legs and stout feet—important characteristics of a good trail or endurance horse. And trusting a good horse out in the wild to stay calm when encountering wild animals and steep slopes is paramount to safety and enjoyment. Appaloosa horses were bred to meet the needs of trail-riding adventurists.

"Some of my best childhood memories," one Appaloosa trail rider shares, "are standing quietly under a huge pine tree waiting for a spring rainfall to pass. I recall my horse's breath against my palm and her eyes half-closed and dreamy. The rhythmic drip of the rain permeated through the forest canopy to the soft pine-needle

2006 Chief Joseph Trail Ride. Photo by Kristen Reiter.

floor beneath me. To this day the smell of wet pine needles and a damp horse call up feelings of peace, simplicity, and tranquility. Whenever I think of those moments, I seem to re-create a sense of purpose in my life."

On a trail ride, it is easy to imagine yourself a rider from long ago, before automobiles existed. Think back when horses were the only means to deliver mail. Imagine riding back in the days when horses meant utility, mobility, and freedom— when they met such vital needs in our day-to-day lives. Imagine following the same trail that the Nez Perce Indians followed through the rugged Northwest mountains 130 years ago as they fled from the U.S. Cavalry. Imagine living like Lewis and Clark or Daniel Boone, free from the worries that we face every day. Imagine riding deep into the wilderness, away from the anxieties and fast pace of our busy life. Before long our anxieties slowly slough away and the really important things in life begin to take shape: peace, gratefulness, beauty, a connection with nature and your horse. A renewed sense of purpose about life.

> The only way to see what God made is from the back of a horse.
> —CHARLES M. RUSSELL

"I recall coming upon some of the most amazing sights," another trail rider recalls. "More than once I'd see herds of elk that were not at all afraid of my horse. We'd nonchalantly wander closer to the herd to see what they'd do, and they often just raised their heads a little to look at us, then kept grazing. Other times we came across porcupines in the pea fields, snapping away at the spring crops, coyotes that always kept a skeptical distance, and many, many deer, often with fawns at their sides. My most fond memory, though, was the day I rode upon a newborn fawn, still wet from birth. I'll never forget how I felt watching it struggle to its feet and wobble after its mother across a shallow trench. I really regret that I didn't have a camera."

Avid trail riders would agree that trail riding is contagious—that once the open air is in your blood, you can't help but long for it. Thoreau understood the

Kyle Kimple with Wrangler's Neon. Photo by Jan Bard, Bar-D Ranch, Maple Valley, Washington.

power of nature and its ability to drive us back to our more primal roots where life makes more sense. "That man is the richest whose pleasures are the cheapest," he said, and "all good things are wild and free."

"Trail riding is a mystic experience," exclaims addicted trail rider Bob Swick of Lebanon, Missouri. "It's deep and spiritual and mysterious. It's hard to explain unless you've been there and felt that incredible oneness with nature and your horse."

Mary Sue Kunz of Las Vegas, Nevada, says, "Appaloosas have been a great joy to my husband and me since 1971 when we fell in love with our first one, a great behemoth of a horse called Plaudit Domino. His nickname, however, was Rock. It suited him. Because of Rock, we had to have more Appaloosas, and so began our spotted journey. We raised a few over the years, standing our own Reserve World Champion stallion, The Shootist, who gave us extremely agile babies who could do anything under saddle. I still ride one of Shooter's colts, the best horse I ever rode, Smith & Wesson, now 26 and still going strong. I have ridden the entire Chief Joseph Trail on my Appaloosas. Heza Tough Cinch, or 'Tuffy,' and I just rode the rough Yosemite backcountry for a week—a place you don't take just any horse."

> Appaloosas make the good places better.
>
> —MARY SUE KUNZ

The Trail Gait

Many trail riders value the Indian shuffle gait in their Appaloosa as much or more than they value its color or its spots or its incredible endurance. While not considered valuable in the show world, trail and endurance riders find the smooth, rolling gait, characteristic of many foundation Appaloosas, one of its most prized birthrights.

It wasn't until the Nez Perce Appaloosa became the horse of ranchers and cowboys that the unique gait became dubbed the "Indian shuffle." Many foundation Appaloosas came by the gait naturally when the Appaloosa Horse Club was first formed in 1938. Contemporary breeders who stay as close to foundation stock as possible can maintain a greater percentage of Indian shufflers in their herd. The trait appears to be dominant in Appaloosa-to-Appaloosa breedings when one parent has it, but crossing to other breeds tends to eliminate the gait fairly quickly.

As a matter of fact, over the years the Indian shuffle has become more and more difficult to find.

Many breeders, however, breed specifically for the gait—particularly those who breed for long-distance and endurance riding. Since the gait requires minimum effort on the part of the horse, proves highly sure-footed in hilly country, and offers the rider a smooth, quick pace, it is often the trait of choice for veteran long-distance riders.

Trail Riding Conformation

Show ring trends have affected the Appaloosa's conformation overall. The success of Appaloosas with Quarter Horse breeding has resulted in many registered Appaloosas that are more Quarter Horse than Appaloosa. The pedigrees of many successful show horses often contain very few foundation Appaloosas in their lineage.

Years ago, however, the Appaloosa's conformation was distinctive and distinguishable from other breeds. A compact body; deep chest; long sloping shoulders and pasterns; muscular thighs; and straight, lean head, combined with its colorful markings, made the Appaloosa stand out. These athletic characteristics are what contemporary foundation Appaloosa breeders continue to strive for. Characteristics that are important and useful on the trail, like stout legs and feet, are not valued in the show ring. Thus, two separate veins of Appaloosa breeding continue, depending upon the desired end use for the horse. While these two separate breed lines might seem contradictory in nature, they actually serve to raise awareness of the Appaloosa's versatile potential.

Although the show ring is dominated by contemporary Appaloosas with different conformation from the foundation-bred Appaloosas, the show-bred Appaloosa still claims amazing versatility and beauty, excelling in western pleasure, western horsemanship, and halter classes as well as calf roping, reining, cutting, side saddle, pleasure driving, hunter under saddle, and open jumper—to name a few.

Appaloosa trail horses, for the most part, exemplify the Nez Perce horse of the early 19th century. Ranging in size from 14 to 16 hands, these sturdy horses

2006 Chief Joseph Trail Ride. Photo by Kristen Reiter.

out-perform other breeds on the trail. During endurance races, which require a fast pace for 25 to 100 miles, Appaloosas nearly always check in with lower pulse rates than other breeds.

Sponsored Appaloosa Trail Rides

Organized trail rides are a splendid way to incorporate horseback riding into your summer vacation. These trail rides usually provide food for both riders and horses, in addition to boarding facilities, lodging, and a huge network of horse-lovers to become acquainted with. These organized rides can be found worldwide.

Red Wing Two Moons, 2006 Chief Joseph Trail Ride. Photo by Kevin Pullen.

The Appaloosa Horse Club sponsors four annual trail rides in different regions of the United States each year—all weeklong events that proffer the country's most spectacular scenery, combined with a strong dose of history on horseback. Three of the organized rides maintain a base camp that riders return to each day following their trail ride, while one, the Chief Joseph, moves to a new campsite every night.

Riders follow trails made by Indians, outlaws, and famous Old West settlers and experience the outdoors firsthand along with their favorite horse, family members, and friends. Not only is the daily scenery spectacular and the adventures exciting and unpredictable, evenings are accented by great food, music, dancing, games, and entertainment. The camaraderie established among trail riders keeps many coming back year after year. The wholesome life lessons learned on the trail from nature, horses, and friendship can contribute to a whole new attitude towards life.

The most popular and prestigious Appaloosa Horse Club–sponsored ride is the Chief Joseph Trail Ride, which follows the path that Chief Joseph and his Nez Perce band trod during the war of 1877 as they fled from the U.S. Cavalry to avoid eviction from their land. The 1,300-mile trail ride began in 1965, organized by George

Over 200 horses and riders traveled the 2006 Chief Joseph Trail. Photo by Kristen Reiter.

Hatley and Don Johnson, who wanted to provide Appaloosa owners an opportunity to experience the history of the horse firsthand. Riders from all over the world convene each year in this beautiful, historic land to show their reverence for the Appaloosa horse and the tribe that bred it into existence. All riders are required to use registered Appaloosa horses—a tribute to the history of the ride for

Trail riders take a break. Photo by Kristen Reiter.

certain, but also as a safety precaution. Appaloosas can handle the steep canyons and rocky terrain better than other breeds.

In 1976 a bill was passed to study the historic Nez Perce Trail, pushed through by George Hatley. Sharon Saare, of Bethoud, Colorado, came up with the idea of the Nez Perce Trail becoming a National Trail and provided written testimony for the U.S. Senate hearings, gaining the necessary support for legislation in both houses of Congress. As a result, in 1986 the trail was designated as part of the National Trails System, and in 1991 a ceremony took place, dedicating it as the Nez Perce National Historic Trail.

The logo that marks the trail depicts Appaloosas. "I wanted Appaloosas used on the logo because it would positively identify the trail as the Nez Perce Trail," says Hatley. A Nez Perce prayer was offered up at the dedication by Nez Perce Indians Horace Axtell and Joe Redthunder.

One Nez Perce said, "We look upon the trail as a cemetery, as we buried our people the full length of it. Our people recognize its significance. Many of our people died and were buried we know not where on this trail. This dedication is for our future children, as this trail will be here forever."

Mike Croy, 2006 Chief Joseph Trail Ride. Photo by Kevin Pullen.

The Nez Perce National Historic Trail meanders across four states: Idaho, Montana, Wyoming, and Oregon. It begins near the remote Wallowa Valley town of Joseph, Oregon, and ends near Bear Paw in north central Montana, where Chief Joseph finally surrendered to the U.S. Cavalry. It was here, just a short distance from the Canadian border and safety, that the tribe's select Appaloosa horses were taken by the cavalry and dispersed, putting an abrupt end to the tribe's exceptional equine breeding program. There is no doubt that the superiority of the horses contributed to the tribe's ability to elude the cavalry for as long as it did.

Some of the Chief Joseph Trail has hardly been altered since 1877. Wagon wheel ruts trench deep into the hot, dry land, reminding riders of the trade route that snaked through the wilderness, of the tribe's difficult escape, and of those who did not survive. The majority of Chief Joseph's tribe was made up of women and children who relied on their hardy Appaloosas to carry them across treacherous rocky canyons and ravines.

Of particular interest to Chief Joseph Trail riders is the Lolo Trail, a section of the trail that follows the route used by Lewis and Clark, the Nez Perce, and General

Don Bradshaw of Clearfield, Utah, 2006 Chief Joseph Trail Ride. Photo by Kevin Pullen.

Howard. Later the trail was used to move goods between Idaho and Montana, following the high crest of a ridge between two drainages. Trail riders encounter breathtaking mountain scenery. To look back over your shoulder and see a string of 200 Appaloosas snaking across the ridge is one of the most meaningful, living illustrations of the heart of the Chief Joseph Trail Ride.

It takes 13 years to complete the entire Chief Joseph Trail, and several riders have completed it more than once. As a matter of fact, some have been on every single ride since 1965. What keeps them coming back? The people, the horses, the beautiful land, the challenge. But most of all, a deep respect for the Appaloosa horse and its amazing history.

They now knew why their Appaloosas were surefooted and untiring, having traveled across the country that demanded such characteristics. They developed a keen appreciation of Joseph's love for the land that had belonged to him and his fathers before him, and they had recaptured some of the romance, heroism, and tragedy of his Nez Perce War of 1877.

—GEORGE HATLEY, *RIDING THE NEZ PERCE WAR TRAIL TWICE*

Beauty Is More than Skin Deep

By Kristin Reiter, DVM

Winter had finally released its sodden hold on the residents of the Pacific Northwest. I caught a whiff of moistened earth and fresh grass...spring was in the air. My gelding smelled it too, for he raised his head and flicked his ear at the same time I inhaled and closed my eyes. It was the perfect day for a trail ride. ◆ *I squinted as my eyes adjusted to the dramatic change from light to dark as I emerged from the barn. In front of me stood three equine silhouettes, their heads held high and their tails dragging the ground. One mare side-stepped as I joined the group, her dainty feet dancing atop the gravel. Another nickered, tossing his thick mane as he nodded his head. I turned to my gelding. His mane was groomed and trimmed to a length of three inches and his tail, though somewhat lengthy, was not, by any means, thick. I was definitely the minority in the group...a sole Appaloosa tagging along with a herd of Morgan horses.* ◆ *As we walked along, I endured stereotypical accusations about undesirable traits of Appaloosa horses and why Morgans were far superior mounts. My comrades made comments about how, were it not for his coat, an Appaloosa really was boring and plain. My horse quietly plodded along the trail with his head hung low and eyes half-closed. I could understand why they would arrive at such a conclusion, but I knew the beauty of my horse was more than skin deep. If only I could be offered the chance to provide them with a demonstration.* ◆ *I could never have predicted that my hopes would become reality within the first thirty minutes of our ride. The trail we'd chosen meandered through the trees, bordered on both sides by dense ferns and rotting, moss-covered logs. Despite the recent rains we'd had, the trail was firm beneath our horses' feet. As they quietly walked along, we shared stories of our varied equine experiences. Suddenly, our conversations were interrupted by an onslaught of intense chattering and scratching.* ◆ *I studied the canopy of cedar boughs above us, but couldn't locate what I had assumed was a disrupted brown squirrel. Our lead rider shifted her seat in the saddle and pointed above her head to the left, "There it is!"* ◆ *Her mare, being well-schooled and sensitive to changes in leg pressure and shifts of body weight, mistook her gesture as a request to sidepass. She obediently sidestepped off the compressed soil of the trodden trail and into the fern grove beside us. While the soil on the trail was tamped solid from years of use, the ground surrounding it consisted of moss and decaying plant life that now soaked up the water from the recent rainfall like a thirsty sponge. I watched in disbelief as the massive mare shrunk instantly to pony height.* ♦ *The mare panicked with her loss of footing and began to thrash wildly. Every lurch caused her to sink deeper in the muck. Soon, her neck was lathered in sweat and her respiration was labored. She gathered herself and then hurdled her body forward, but the effort was futile. She fell to her knees, belly-deep in peat and muck...exhausted.* ♦ *With the frightened mare temporarily quieted, her rider determined it was now safe, and necessary, to dismount. She swung her leg over the mare's rump and gripped the saddle as she lowered herself into the clammy bog.* ♦ *In the meantime, the mare behind me grew impatient with inactivity. She threw her head up and danced sideways. When her back end plunged into the softer soil, she exploded! She scrambled to return to the trail, but her front feet joined the rear and there were now two terrified Morgans entrapped in the quagmire.* ♦ *The third rider dismounted his gelding, looped its reins over his arm, and rushed to assist his wife. When he approached, her mare suddenly shifted her weight and bumped him with her shoulder. While attempting to regain his balance, he tripped on a log and fell, pulling on the reins in his descent. Thus far, his gelding had been safe on high ground. With the tug on his reins, he dutifully followed his master and joined the others in the swamp.* ♦ *As pandemonium exploded around me, I dismounted my gelding to lend assistance. I dropped my reins and commanded him to "stand" as I'd done routinely in training for arena trail competition. He dropped his head and cocked a rear foot in relaxation, taking advantage of the break.* ♦ *The husband and wife team behind me worked together to free their duo as I helped my friend clamber out and encourage her mare to do the same. All the while, my Appaloosa stood quietly, studying the scene with mild interest.* ♦ *With Morgans and riders restored to solid ground, cold, wet, and covered in muck, we made the unanimous decision to return home. I remounted my horse and maneuvered him in a tight turn, manipulating his forehand and haunches to move simultaneously so we could remain on firm footing. We waited as the others redirected their horses for home. One mare circled too wide and plunged, once again, into the bog. She threw herself forward and back onto the trail, but not without striking her rider's leg with*

Aleshia Lundgren, 2006 Chief Joseph Trail Ride. Photo by Kevin Pullen.

her hoof. ◆ *Finally, my friends had mounted their horses—wet, bruised, and soiled. It wasn't until then that they realized that my horse was as pristine as when I led him from the aisle, and I had survived the experience with nary a mark. Their saddles would require cleaning, their pads were drenched, one rider had lost a spur, and it was unlikely the stains would ever come out of their jeans.* ◆ *I held my head high on our ride home and relished in their defeat. The Morgan aficionados learned a valuable lesson that day...the quality of the Appaloosa penetrates deep beneath the colorful hide, for they are also strong of heart and sound of mind.*

The Appaloosa horse can make your trail riding dreams come true. Truly an amazing horse, the Appaloosa embodies the heart of the great outdoors: rugged, dependable, beautiful, and calm, it has all that any rider needs to venture to places where man rarely goes. Chief Joseph and his tribe, through selective breeding practices, created a horse fit to trek the roughest terrain. With the Wallowa Valley pulsing through its veins, the Appaloosa's heart and mind are as big as its legacy. ℭℓℯ

Dick Roth (left) and Joe Bard with Wrangler's Neon. Photo by Jan Bard, Bar-D Ranch, Maple Valley, Washington.

Cowboy gear. Photo by Kristen Reiter.

The Warning. Photo by Jessica Wright.

At Work and Play

Performance

The aim of teaching a horse to move beneath you is to remind him how he moved when he was free.

—Henry Taylor, *The Flying Change*

Appaloosas are natural competitors and hearty, willing workers. Some have been bred for specific competitive events like racing, jumping, and cutting cattle, but most are very willing partners in anything they're asked to do. As a matter of fact, many people are pleasantly surprised at the versatility of the Appaloosa. Show records reveal that Appaloosas have the ability to compete against other breeds at top levels. Appaloosas are also commonly used in a variety of venues, from ranch work to hunting to therapeutic riding.

Leopard gelding owned by Roy Scoles, Gramps Appaloosas, Princeton, Idaho. Photo by Jason Abbott.

Christine Nelson riding Ristow at an open breed show in Princeton, Idaho. Photo by Kevin Pullen.

The quiet, competitive spirit of the Appaloosa is only one of the major reasons that Appaloosa owners show their horses. Combine that spirit with athleticism and color, and the show ring lights up with interest.

Equine competitors embody winning characteristics like passion, the ability to focus and be trained, and the desire to please and listen closely to cues. It all comes down to spirit, really. There's nothing more satisfying for Appaloosa owners to experience from their horse than that deep-down desire and ability to win, resulting from a close camaraderie that denotes a winning team.

Showing

The Appaloosa Horse Club sponsors a variety of classes for showcasing the talent, athleticism, and diversity of their breed that includes regional, national, and world opportunities to compete. Because Appaloosas also compete well against other breeds, the ApHC's Appaloosa Competitive All-Breed Activities Program promotes and rewards those Appaloosas that excel in all-breed competitions outside of the ApHC-sponsored events. This includes shows, trail rides, and races, providing the opportunity and recognition in open competitions that are offered by communities worldwide.

Christine Nelson riding Ristow at an open breed show in Princeton, Idaho. Photo by Kevin Pullen.

The Appaloosa Horse Club's National and World championship shows include over 200 classes that incorporate a wide range of age groups and disciplines. In addition to western and English classes, the shows include events that reflect the Northwest history and tradition of the horse, like the most colorful at halter class, which awards the horse with the most correct conformation and brilliant color; the heritage class; the Nez Perce stake race; the Camas Prairie stump race; steer daubing; and the rope race.

The heritage class requires competitors to dress in costumes that depict the history of the horse. Each costume piece should be an original or an authentic replica of an original. During the class, each competitor is given a chance to explain their costume pieces and the history he or she represents.

Open breed show, Caldwell, Idaho. Photo by Jeri Rainer.

The Nez Perce stake race and the Camas Prairie stump race are inspired by the games played by the Nez Perce when exhibiting their riding skills. In the Nez Perce stake race, two horses race around poles on identical courses laid side by side. The winner moves up the bracket to race other winners.

The Camas Prairie stump race is designed after a barrel race, but differs in that two horses race against each other on identical circuits opposite the start/finish line. The riders start beside each other going opposite directions, and the first horse and rider back across the line wins the race.

Marge Bibeau riding A&B Skips, owned by Marge and Julie Bibeau, heritage class, 2006 Appaloosa National Youth Show. Photo by Jennie Wandler.

Barrel racing. Photo by Larry Williams Photography.

Steer daubing is similar to steer wrestling, except the rider does not dismount. Instead, the rider carries a stick with chalk on the tip and marks the steer within a designated area on its side. Once the rider marks the steer, the stick is raised in the air to stop the clock.

The rope race is similar to musical chairs. Riders line up on the start line, then run their horses to a row of ropes that are hung from a wire across the opposite end of the arena. There is always one less rope than number of competitors, and the rider who does not get hold of a rope is eliminated. This is repeated until there is only one horse left.

In addition to its unique games classes, in 1998 the Appaloosa Horse Club began a new leadline class for challenged riders—something that no other horse club offers. This class allows physically and mentally challenged riders the opportunity to compete. During the first year of the competition, riders traveled from all across the U.S. to take part, and since then the class has become highly popular.

English-style riding initially became especially popular in the eastern United States, where people hunted on horseback and rode as a social activity. Appaloosas compete in a variety of English classes like jumping, which is judged on manners, style,

Rachel Pozzi, 2006 National Youth Show. Photo by Diane Rice.

flow of strides, and balance; English equitation, which is judged on the rider's form; and hunter under saddle, where the rider works the horse at three gaits and is judged on the smoothness of the horse's gait, its free-flowing stride, and its willingness to perform.

While some horses and riders compete in both English and western events at the shows, taller horses excel in English events, where elegance and smooth, balanced movement is a plus. Apparel for the English rider includes a traditional-style hunt cap, a fitted jacket, shirt, jodhpurs or breeches, and tall boots. The English saddle and tack is lighter and simpler than western, fitting the rider close to the horse.

Appaloosa stallion All Hands On Zip exceled in English events. Standing 17 hands

English riding. Photo by Daria Killinger, Equiscape Photography.

Sara E. Michalak on Spotted Image, Old River Ranch, Harvard, Idaho. Photo by Kevin Pullen.

tall, "Jack" displayed the modern flowing movement that collected awards in hunter under saddle events. During his show career from 1995 to 1999, the stallion won multiple national and world titles, including 1999 world champion stallion hunter in hand and world champion master's non-pro hunter under saddle. His foals have also

Sara E. Michalak on Spotted Image, Old River Ranch, Harvard, Idaho. Photo by Kevin Pullen.

become notable winners in English events in both the U.S. and Europe, earning him second place in the Appaloosa Horse Club's leading sires of performance horses.

Western riding began out of necessity on cattle ranches because cowboys were required to cut calves from a herd to rope, wrestle, and brand. The western show classes are styled after these types of ranching activities, where a quick, well-trained horse is paramount to success.

Cutting

In cutting competition, the rider moves into a herd and parcels out one cow, moves it away from the herd, then keeps the horse between the cut cow and the herd. Once the horse is focused on the cow, the rider drops the reins and lets the horse take over. The cow tries hard to return to the herd, and a well-trained cutting horse mirrors the cow's movement. If the cow stands still, some cutting horses will get low to the ground and tremble, waiting for the cow's next move. Cutting competitions last two minutes and thirty seconds. If the rider determines that the cut cow is "bad," or non-cooperative, he is free to let the cow go and choose another from the herd.

Docs Hickory Doll, an Appaloosa daughter by the legendary stallion Ima Doc O'Lena, represents four generations of Appaloosa cutting horses that are owned by the Smith family of Geary, Oklahoma. "I like these horses and I like this bloodline," says Wade Smith. "I don't want to ride anything else."

Photo by Daria Killinger, Equiscape Photography.

Docs Hickory Doll won the non-pro cutting world championship in 2005 while in foal to Smart Little Lena (AQHA). Because of her pregnancy, Wade had considered not taking the mare, but decided to at the last minute. The fact that she won the championship showcases the phenomenal spirit and talent of the Smiths' Appaloosa cutting-horse bloodlines. Not only that, their horses are expected

Photo by Daria Killinger, Equiscape Photography.

Cutting competition. Photo by Larry Williams Photography.

to work on their 200-head cattle ranch when they're not showing. "It's really important to us that our show horses get used at home and in the show pen," Wade says.

Liz Kinkaid is another competitor who vows that Appaloosas are top-notch competitors. Her horses, Gay Bars Silver and Docs Rose Field, are both champions in the cutting show pen. "I've been extremely blessed," Liz says when talking about "Silver," her stallion who was foaled to 19-year-old mare Silver Roxie in 2000. "I couldn't have created a better horse if I had molded one out of clay."

Team Roping

Team roping involves a header and a heeler to rope the front and hind ends of a steer. Team roping competitions begin with a steer in a chute and the ropers on horseback to each side. The steer is released from the chute and given a head start down the arena, about 10 to 15 feet, after which point the ropers may give chase. The header comes up on the steer's left side and ropes it around the horns or neck, securing the rope around the saddle horn, then steers his horse to the left across the arena, pulling the steer behind him. The heeler follows the steer and ropes its hind feet. The heeler finishes the run by stopping his horse while simultaneously dallying his rope around his saddle horn. A team-roping event averages 5 to 15 seconds, and the team that performs their job the quickest wins the event.

In 2003 header Nick Sartain of Yukon, Oklahoma, and his 12-year-old Appaloosa mare Really Elegant were on their way to success in the professional ranks of team roping when they qualified for the Wrangler National Finals Rodeo in Las Vegas in 2004, where they ranked 23rd in the world. At the Denver rodeo earlier that year, Nick had won the fastest time with four seconds flat.

Really Elegant, owned and raised by Nick's grandmother, is a well-trained, versatile horse who is fast and responsive. "She fits me perfectly and is consistent. She is the best horse I have—my favorite one," says Nick.

"Nick just absolutely depends on her," says Nick's dad, Terry. "He saves her for when the chips are down and he's got to go. She's out of the box fast and gets up on a steer fast."

Nick started out as a boy participating in dummy roping contests at the National Appaloosa Show every year. In addition to his success at the National Finals rodeo, he won the 1999 International Professional Rodeo Association (IPRA) and 2000 Professional Rodeo Cowboys Association (PRCA) Rookie of the Year awards. In 2006 he won the Wrangler ProRodeo Tour Round at the San Angelo Stock Show and Rodeo.

Reining

In reining competitions, the horse and rider perform a complex pattern of circles, spins, roll backs, and dramatic sliding stops—all with cues that are nearly invisible to the spectator. Some top reining horses can perform without a bridle, an impressive demonstration of sensitivity and intellect where the rider cues the horse entirely with leg and seat pressure. In early reining competitions, a thread was often tied between the bit and the reins to see what horse and rider could perform without breaking the thread. In other words, the best reiners performed using very little to no rein. When performing freestyle, contemporary reiners often ride without a bridle to showcase their horse's talent.

In a roll back, the horse lopes in a straight line, stops and spins on his hindquarters, and lopes back on the exact same line. This move requires extreme athleticism and controlled movement. To spin, the horse pivots on his hindquarters, moving the

front legs in a circle at an amazingly quick pace. Sliding stops are often a spectator favorite, where the horse, from a full gallop, tucks his hindquarters underneath himself and slides to a stop in an impressive cloud of dust.

Terry Thompson is most interested in a horse with heart. A top trainer in National Reining Horse Association, American Quarter Horse Association, and Appaloosa Horse Club competitions, Terry has been in the industry for over 30 years and has over 210 National and World titles to his credit. In 1977 he won an open

Top and *bottom:* Terry Thompson. Photos by Richard Reed.

reining competition at the Quarter Horse Congress on an Appaloosa named Charger-Charmer, and in 1986 placed fourth in the National Reining Horse Association Futurity on a 1983 Appaloosa mare named Gunsmokes Skeeter. Both awards

Top and *bottom*: Ima Smokin Frosty, owned by Shawn and Tracy Reynolds, ridden by Terry Thompson. Photos by Richard Reed.

were the highest-placing awards ever by an Appaloosa in that class. Terry later rode a loud-colored stallion named The Miracle Chip to win the Solid Gold and Appaloosa National and World titles in 2-year-old western pleasure, all in the year 1992, another unmatched feat.

At the Appaloosa World Show in 2001, Terry took the opportunity to salute the New York City firemen and heroes of the World Trade Center disaster just a few weeks earlier. That year, the freestyle competition boasted 18 entries, with almost half of them displaying patriotic or heroic themes. It was a sign of the times—people were deeply moved by the tragic events that had taken place in New York City, Washington, D.C., and Pennsylvania. They were in need of ways to express their empathy for the families of the men, women, and children who lost their lives. Terry dedicated his freestyle routine to the memory of his father, G. L. Thompson, who had recently passed away.

Terry borrowed a fireman's suit from the local fire department, and he and Ima Frosty Lena brought the *standing-room-only* crowd to its feet during the routine. The awe-inspiring creativity of the music and the high-caliber, bridleless maneuvers by "Frosty" earned the duo the bronze trophy for the event.

During the performance, Terry's crew wore tee shirts that displayed the New York Fire Department logo. Proceeds from the shirts went to benefit the New York Fire Department. Photographer Larry Williams captured a reverent moment at the end of the routine, which saluted the world's heroes. This picture became the cover of the January 2002 *Appaloosa Journal* issue. A framed and matted copy was sent to the NY Fire Department in appreciation of their tireless dedication.

"I wanted to do something," Terry said. "After everything that had gone on that year, it just seemed appropriate."

O for a horse with wings!

—WILLIAM SHAKESPEARE

Endurance Racing

Endurance riding is a strenuous long-distance horse race, requiring the horse to complete, at the top levels, 100 miles in 10 to 12 hours. Arabian horses generally dominate the top levels, but any breed can compete.

Endurance horses are regularly checked by veterinarians along the riding course for soundness, dehydration, and pulse rate. As a matter of fact, no other equine sport requires such close observation of the horse—a testimony in itself of the extreme fitness level required to compete. To continue the ride, the horse must pass the exam, with a reduced heart rate of 64 beats per minute before continuing. Any horse deemed unfit by the veterinarian to continue is eliminated from the race.

Endurance riding is a worldwide sport, particularly popular in hot and arid areas of the world. In some countries, the winner of an endurance race is determined by a combination of speed and the recovery rate of the horse. In other countries, awards are presented to any horse and rider that achieved a required standard.

Endurance riding is governed by the International Federation for Equestrian Sports (FEI), which establishes rules and regulations with the welfare of the horse as top priority. The most well-known American 100-mile endurance ride is The Western States Trail Ride in California, popularly called The Tevis Cup.

In 2006 the Appaloosa Horse Club started a National Championship Appaloosa Endurance Ride in conjunction with a ride open to all breeds of horses. The top Appaloosa in the inaugural 50-mile National Championship Endurance Ride, which took place on June 3, 2006, in Palmyra, Wisconsin, was Fourmile's Kashtin, ridden by Dawn Haas of Eagle, Wisconsin. Dawn and Fourmile's Kashtin also took top honors for conditioning, winning the George Hatley Cup for the Appaloosa with the best condition at the end of the race. Taking second place was Varre Blackcherry, ridden by Jeffery Hartman of Huntington, Pennsylvania. Third place went to DKG Midnight Lace and rider Laurie Durbin of Winfield, Missouri.

Appaloosas have excelled in endurance racing for years. Peter and Penny Toft of Queensland, Australia, have competed worldwide on their Appaloosa-Arab Electra BP Murdoch. The Tofts breed endurance horses and market them to top-level competitors worldwide. Racing twice at the elite Tevis Cup in California, Murdoch and Peter placed fourth and sixth in a mix of about 200 other horses of various breeds.

"What we look for in a good endurance horse is conformation and athletic ability—we like them to have a good length of rein, and attitude is very important," says Penny. "Electra BP Murdoch is our best endurance horse."

"'Tough' is the best word to describe Murdoch," says Peter. "He's proven to be a sound horse with phenomenal recoveries."

Blue Ribbon Downs, Sallisaw, Oklahoma. Finishing first in the 39th Running of the Cricket Bars Appaloosa Futurity was the colt Moon Bully out of the mare Fancy Moon and by the stallion Man With The Power. Moon Bully is owned by Steve and Kati Neal of Eufaula, Oklahoma, and is trained by J. D. Anderson of Sallisaw and Tahlequa. Veteran jockey Rodger Smith rode the 330 yards in 17.33 seconds over a muddy track. Photo by Gene Wilson & Associates.

Racing

Appaloosa racehorses continue to set and break many all-breed records. Known as middle-distance runners, Appaloosas are fierce and fast competitors in the racing industry, competing in distances from 220 yards to eight furlongs (one mile). Racing is a contagious sport; there are more than 500 Appaloosa racehorses receiving over $3,000,000 annually. Following are some Appaloosa racing statistics that tell the story.

1976: Appaloosa We Go Easy beat the Thoroughbred Right Pocket in a $20,000 match race at Detroit Race Course.

1982: Appaloosa champion Undercover Willie beat the Thoroughbred Grey Moon Runner in an $8,000 winner-take-all match race at the Valley Race Meet in California.

1986: Appaloosa Blowing Easy won the first $100,000 race in California, which was the richest purse for any breed on the Northern California Fair Circuit.

1989: Appaloosa Wing It became the first horse to win the Golden Stakes Incentive Award by winning the 1989 Star of Stars Futurity and coming back in 1990 to win the California Derby.

Moon Bully in the Winner's Circle, Blue Ribbon Downs, Sallisaw, Oklahoma.
Photo by Gene Wilson & Associates.

1991: Appaloosa Very Easy won the Battle of the Breeds at Remington Park, beating the Quarter Horse Heavenly Smash and the Paint Rollin La Ree.

1995: Appaloosa Apache Double, one of the first Appaloosa racehorses to earn a medallion, became the all-time leading sire of money earners, with totals of $2,032,998.

2001: Making Ends Meet was the only Appaloosa in the Quarter Horse Handicap at the Western Montana Fair. He took the top honors with a two-length win in a full field of eight and broke the old Appaloosa track record set by MS Native Charge in 1984. Making Ends Meet has track records all over the country in distances ranging from 350 to 770 yards.

2005: Appaloosas won 17 races in June, held in California, Colorado, Idaho, and Oklahoma, and three all-breed stakes races in July. The races covered 350 to 870 yards. Natural Queen won the 35-yard Western States Futurity in Aurora, Colorado, by a length. You R My Sunshine won the Lewis Wartchow Memorial in Tulsa, Oklahoma. Hand Me Your Chips took home close to $3,500 in winnings at the Southern Belle and overcame 22 other horses to come out on top.

Wing It

Wing It, one of the most legendary Appaloosa racehorses of all time, was foaled in 1987 in Nocona, Texas. Sired by ApHC Hall of Fame racehorse Bull Nunnelly and out of the Thoroughbred mare Damascus Honey, Wing It's owner, Bill Jones, had low expectations for the colt because he was so thin and gangly. As a yearling, Wing It was gelded and sent to Henry Smith in California for training, in hopes that he would bring the $5,000 asking price. No one saw potential enough in the colt to purchase him, but as Jones and Smith worked with him, they noticed the colt gaining more balance. ◆ *In 1989, still hoping to sell Wing It, Smith trailered*

The Legendary Appaloosa

him, along with six other 2-year-olds, to Vallejo, California, where all were slated to run 4 furlongs (990 yards) in the Vallejo Futurity. ◆ On race day, Wing It rocketed out of the gates in the trials. Both Smith and Jones were floored as they watched the colt fly by the rest of the field and close in on the finish line with a five-length lead. Wing It repeated his performance in the finals. ◆ For the next six years, Wing It had an amazing race career, setting track records that held for years, finally wrapping it up as an 11-year-old at Remington Park in Oklahoma City in 1998, where he finished in the money. Among his accolades, Wing It became the first Appaloosa to win a mixed breed stakes race when he won the Los Alamitos Handicap in 1992, running against the AQHA's distance champion and Cowboy Hall of Fame inductee Griswold. ◆ Bill Jones sent Wing It back to Nocona, Texas, to trainer Bob Gilbert for the 1992-1994 race seasons, where he ran against some of the world's best Quarters Horses, Paints,

and Thoroughbreds at the handicaps and stakes races. Wing It made a name for himself that endures among race fans to this day. Gilbert knew Wing It was a great runner the first day, when he saw the racehorse power out of the turns. ◆ Noting his outstanding race talent, a noted Thoroughbred racing barn proposed a match race between Wing It and a Thoroughbred. The half-mile race was set for the Del Mar Race Course in California with a $100,000 purse. But 30 days before the race, the Thoroughbred promoters canceled, claiming that if a Thoroughbred was beaten by an Appaloosa, it would destroy their reputation. ◆ Wing It retired to Nocona, where he spent several years with other retired racehorses, until Bill Jones's death in August 1995. Victoria Ennis of Kingston, Oklahoma, was then asked to take over his care. Victoria, a noted Appaloosa breeder and owner of several Hall of Fame champions of her own, agreed, claiming that Wing It is now a bit spoiled with 40 acres of pasture and numerous broodmares to keep company. "He acts as if this treatment is his birthright," she says. And who are we to argue with a champion?

Tom O'Brien and Proud Reflection, Old River Ranch, Harvard, Idaho.
Photo by Jason Abbott.

Racing Fate

By Victoria Ennis

My career with Appaloosas and racing all started with a barrel horse named Turquoise Splash and a woman by the name of Lily Caldwell. I worked for Lily as an apprentice jockey for her mostly un-broke barrel and race horses, and I'll always be thankful for what she taught me and for her influence on my life today.

◆ *As the only Appaloosa Lily had in her barn, Turquoise quickly became my favorite horse. Before this, I owned a buckskin mare named Merry Weedo, named by* Equus Magazine *as the "blue hen" producer of Appaloosa western pleasure horses. She was entered into the ApHC Hall of Fame in 1989. I soon purchased Turquoise Splash from Lily, and from there my need for speed included purchasing some race-bred broodmares, including Tulsa Girl, the dam to Turquoise Splash and daughter of Belmont Stakes winner High Echelon. Along with producing Turquoise Splash, Tulsa Girl produced a World Champion open jumper and a National Champion hunter-in-hand stallion.* ◆ *When Lily's husband, Jim, asked me what stallion I would breed my new mares to, I replied that it would be a son of Mr. Spotted Bull. Jim questioned why I would not prefer to simply pay half the price and travel half the distance from our farm to breed to Mr. Spotted Bull himself. I assumed that the old horse was deceased—but not so. Mr. Spotted Bull was 19 years old and just an hour's drive from our place. So that's what I did. When I went to pick up my mares, the gentleman who owned Bull at the time asked if I would consider buying him. He said that Bull deserved to be with an Appaloosa person who would take care of him. I was thrilled and accepted the deal.* ◆ *Turquoise and I ended up winning two World titles in stakes and many top 10 placings in stumps. We also won the San Antonio Livestock Show twice in sold-out performances for horse versus horse competition on poles. Then, the race babies started hitting the ground and headed to the track by the time they were two. It took a few years to get to the winner's circle, where we now expect to frequent. Then, I Love Willie, a grandson of Mr. Spotted Bull, came my way. He has become what Mr. Spotted Bull was tenfold: another great one, with another colorful history.*

It will be a long time before another horse can fill the shoes of either of those two great sires. ◆ *Willie has sired three Supreme Champion racehorses in four years' time, and he has sired the top hunters in the industry, along with leading hunter-in-hand competitors. Never has another stallion sired race, performance, and halter champions (medallion winners) in the same year—and Willie has done it for two years in a row.* ◆ *Where this legacy goes now, we'll have to see. But I think it might have something to do with the young stallions Count Willie, Willies Neon Moon, and Pike Pass. Fate will take us in its funny way where we need to go.*

FIVE STATES HOST APPALOOSA RACING, AS FOLLOWS:

California
Los Alamitos Race Course, Los Alamitos
San Joaquin County Fair, Stockton
Alameda County Fair and Cal-Bred
    Derby, Pleasanton Handicap, Pleasanton
Solano County Fair, Vallejo Futurity,
    Vallejo
Sonoma County Fair, California
    Appaloosa Derby, Santa Rosa
San Mateo County Fair, Cal-Bred
    Futurity, San Mateo
Humbolt County Fair, Ferndale
California State Fair, Sacramento
Fairplex Park, Pomona
Fresno District Fair, Fresno

Idaho
Gem County Fair, Emmett
Les Bois Park, Boise

Pocatello Downs, Pocatello
Sandy Downs, Idaho Falls
Rupert Downs, Rupert
Jerome Racing, Jerome
Oneida County Fair, Malad
Cassia County Fair, Burley
Eastern Idaho State Fair, Blackfoot

Oklahoma
Blue Ribbon Downs, Sallisaw
Remington Park, Oklahoma City
Fair Meadows (County Fair), Tulsa

Texas
Trinity Meadows, Weatherford

Wyoming
Wyoming Downs, Evanston
Central Wyoming Fair, Casper

I will not change my horse with any that treads but on four pasterns...When I bestride him, I soar, I am a hawk. He trots the air, the earth sings when he touches it, the basest horn of his hoofs is more musical than the pipe of Herme...When bestride him I soar, I am a hawk.

—WILLIAM SHAKESPEARE

Open breed show, Caldwell, Idaho. Photo by Jeri Rainer.

Ranching and Rodeo

George Hatley tells the story of an old cowboy named Faye Hubbard, who was a rodeo cowboy from 1925 to 1940. He hit the top of his rodeo career in 1939 when he was a champion bulldogger. ◆ He started rodeoing and stock contracting at a tender age and kept it up until a back injury slowed him down. During 10 years of his stock contracting, he rode an Appaloosa stallion named Ole Rex, bred by Nez Perce Indian Sam Fisher and foaled in about 1928. ◆ Since the rodeo string was shipped over quite a large area of the Northwest and Canada, the blood of Rex was likewise well distributed. Like most Appaloosas, Rex was a versatile horse and was used for about everything a saddle horse can be used for. "We ran wild horses with him in Oregon, 'dogged off him in Canada, roped off him all over the country. He was all around useful," Faye said. ◆ "He was as tough as he was good looking. We used to drive horses from Wilcox to Hay, Washington, which was 40 miles, in less than a day, and he'd still be going strong." ◆ Rex died in 1945 at the age of 28 on Fernie Hubbard's ranch at Harrison, Montana. He sired six foals during his last year. ◆ Folks around Hollywood still remember the Faye and Kay Hubbard Ranch at Van Nuys, California. In Hollywood, Faye did some doubling and stunt work in western movies. He also finished horses. "I'll bet some of those Appaloosas we've been seeing in movies the last couple of years trace to Rex," Faye said. ◆ "Most every cowboy feels a little sentimental about one particular horse that he has owned, some horse that won him a lot of money, or got him out of a tight spot, or just an all-around good, useful horse he rode for a long time," says George. "With Faye, that horse was Rex. In the fall of '47, I rode over to Potlatch, Idaho, for an amateur rodeo where Faye Hubbard was judging. It was about time for the entry and introductions when Faye asked me if he could ride my Appaloosa in the entry, just for old times. ◆ You've never seen an old cowboy look any more proud and pleased than Faye did as he paraded across the arena, paused, and then charged up to the grandstand when his introduction was made. As he rode back, stepped off, and dropped the reins, a few tears slid down his cheeks, and he said, 'I just rode Ole Rex—same rein, same walk.' 'Well, maybe you did in a way,' I answered. 'This old horse's grandmother and Rex came from the same place.'"

Crystal Matthews helping rider Miguel Martinez at Sagebrush Equine Training Center in Eagle, Idaho. Photo by Jason Abbott.

Therapeutic Riding

Therapeutic riding on horseback is a different way of looking at physical therapy because the therapist's tool is a horse, not a swimming pool or other exercise equipment. Therefore, the therapist needs to understand how horses move and what muscle groups the rider will be using.

Persons with disabilities benefit from therapeutic riding in a variety of ways. Increased flexibility and strength are major benefits, not to mention the camaraderie and connection riders make with their horses. The Long Island Riding for the Handicapped Association, Inc. (LIRHA) started in 1978 as a nonprofit organization made up of volunteers who are all North American Riding for the Handicapped Association certified. The mission of the organization, which uses registered Appaloosas, is to provide cost-free therapy on horseback to individuals with physical, emotional, and/or cognitive disabilities; to offer recreation and education with certified riding instructors and licensed physical therapists; to contribute positively to the well-being of students; and to strive to provide these benefits with compassion and in an enjoyable environment, helping students to see their ability—not their disability. Madeline Buglione, the president of LIRHA for 16 years, says, "We may be the only therapeutic riding organization in New York that offers our services for free. Because of it, we now have a four-year waiting list."

Horses trained for therapeutic riding must prove themselves as solid, reliable, bombproof animals, which is why LIRHA uses registered Appaloosas in their program.

Miguel Martinez, therapeutic riding at Sagebrush Equine Training Center in Eagle, Idaho. Photo by Jason Abbott.

Classy

Suzanne Schubert of Dix Hills, New York, has a special relationship with Real Class Act—a therapeutic Appaloosa owned by LIRHA. The bond between Classy and Suzanne became clear to Suzanne's Mom, Nanette ◆ *Suzanne was born with a very rare and severe seizure disorder. Her first stasis grand-mal seizure occurred when she was only 10 months old. What followed were years of tests, medications, and close calls. By the time Suzanne was in the third grade, she was getting strong enough to compete in the New York State Games for the Physically Challenged. While competing, Suzanne spotted some handicapped children riding horses. "Mommy, I want to do that," she said.* ◆ *The next day Nanette called to get Suzanne's name on a two-year waiting list for a therapeutic riding program. By the end of her first 10-week session, Suzanne had improved in muscle tone and strength, but that wasn't the only change. She became more outgoing, more independent; her love for horses gave her confidence in her social life and helped her feel good about herself.* ◆ *One afternoon while riding Classy, Suzanne had a grand-mal seizure. Classy instantly stopped, and stood quietly until help arrived. When a volunteer tried to lead Classy away, the horse resisted, wanting to stay near Suzanne. "He kept trying to walk back to her and you could see his concern for her and that he wanted to be with her," Nanette says.* ◆ *The next week Suzanne returned, and as soon as Classy saw her, he wanted to be near her. "He is always very different when she is riding him, and of course she never wants to ride another horse but the Appaloosa named Classy," says Nanette.*

Sherri Mell of San Antonio, Texas, owns Riding Opportunities Promoting Exceptional Riders (ROPER), another business that uses therapeutic riding for children and adults with disabilities. Sherri is a National Cowgirl Hall of Fame inductee, with more than 100 world and national rodeo and show titles to her name. She is also a Special Olympics volunteer and a physical education teacher at a San Antonio elementary school.

Sherri uses her champion Appaloosas in ROPER, where riders work to their own abilities to increase strength and expedite healing. "The benefits of riding horses are immeasurable for children and adults with disabilities," Sherri says, "including not just physical strength, but a newfound freedom of movement, self-esteem, and camaraderie between horse and rider."

The Appaloosas Sherri uses are bombproof and reliable, with enough intelligence to tune in to any rider's abilities and adjust their movements accordingly. This takes a horse that has incredible stamina as well as that innate sensibility that Appaloosas are so well known for.

Sharlene Adams of Caldwell, Idaho, is a registered NAHRA instructor and works for an organization called Sagebrush Equine Training Center in Eagle, Idaho, that uses Appaloosas. Her love for the Appaloosa horse started when she was around 9 years old, and she now owns four. "I love giving lessons to people with disabilities," Sharlene says.

Sharlene works with a 4-year-old boy who has cerebral palsy. He has a hard time moving his body and is not very verbal. His first few times at the program were very frightening. He was afraid of the horse, and he cried all the time. By his third visit Sharlene had him sitting on the horse in front of her. Over the next few lessons he became more relaxed, and by his last lesson he was smiling, playing games on horseback, and saying "walk" and "I did it!" His grandmother, who said that they had tried pain pills and muscle relaxers but they made him sick, rejoiced that the only thing that relaxed him was horseback riding. "The volunteers and I were in tears of joy," Sharlene says. "I have finally found my calling in life."

Emotional Healers

Many people have turned to horses after an emotional trauma in their life to find that connecting with a horse was just what they needed for healing. "After my divorce, I was lost," says one rider. "So, after years of being horseless, I found the perfect companion—a 10-year-old Appaloosa gelding—who traveled with me down my road to recovery. Getting back to the basics in life really helped: the open fields, the woods, the wild animals. It helps get a person centered again and helped me get back to the roots of who I am and why I'm here. My Appaloosa became my therapist and my best friend."

"There's nothing like going out to the pasture and laying your cheek against the flank of your horse," says writer Claire Davis of Lewiston, Idaho.

Katie Burt and Suspicious Image, Princeton, Idaho. Photo by Kevin Pullen.

Following Claire's emotional divorce, she got back into horses after being away from them for too many years. Her first lesson horse was an Appaloosa. "There is something about the connection between women and horses," she said, "that is hard to explain."

Cancer survivor Jeannie Gibel of Bradenton, Florida, could no longer ride horses because of rheumatoid arthritis, so she decided to get into showing in halter classes. Her friends all owned Appaloosas, and, although she had previously decided to dislike the breed, she was convinced to go look at a weanling Appaloosa show prospect. She fell in love, brought 4-month-old Phoebe home, and trained her at halter. "I absolutely love the Appaloosa breed now," she says. "I can credit this all to Phoebe for turning me around and letting me truly see the Appaloosa for what it is: a beautiful, intelligent, strong, and proud breed, with those big expressive eyes, that anyone would be proud to own." Phoebe's first foal is due in 2007, and Jeannie says she can hardly wait. She is in foal to Invest In My Pizzazz, three-time World and Congress AQHA stallion. He is a grandson of Mr. Conclusion and a great-grandson of Impressive. Phoebe's bloodlines include Goer and Dreamfinder, so Jeannie is expecting a beautiful halter foal.

Real-Life Training

Laurie Loveman of Chagrin Falls, Ohio, was challenged by a stereotype attributed to her Appaloosa. She tells the story of how she and her horse overcame this stereotype and the lessons her friends learned about Appaloosas and life training.

Each day for the 15 years I raised Appaloosa horses, I called my summer-pastured horses in for feeding by hollering, 'Blackie, dinner!' The herd leader, Dakoto Blackie, was a solidly built, 16-hand Appaloosa gelding with enough Thoroughbred in his ancestry to take me anywhere, usually at a speed far greater than I planned on. Blackie had a heart of gold and I trusted him to keep me safe, even at speeds that made the wind shred my hair. ◆ Top Tracy, a daughter of Top Hat H., was the lead mare. Tracy was the youngest of all the horses, but she was tough and no one—except Blackie—ignored her demands. In the pasture, whatever Tracy wanted, Tracy got—the deepest shade, the most succulent grass, the first flat-out nap in the summer sunshine. Tracy wasn't nasty to either horses or people; she just worked to ensure her rank in the herd. She was a smooth riding horse and was just lazy enough that she was safe for my kids to ride. She had great breeding and produced some fine, champion foals. ◆ Our horse farm was relatively peaceful. As the years passed and the mares aged, I stopped breeding them. And then came the first of many sad days when I had to let each horse go to his or her eternal pasture. Then, only Tracy remained, without anyone to boss around except the barn cat. Since I was planning to move to a smaller home with no barn, I found a nice boarding facility for Tracy that had good pastures so she could get exercise if I couldn't ride her. ◆ My only problem with the barn was that Tracy and I were not into dressage like every other boarder. In fact, I often rode Tracy western, even though she had done very well in both English and western pleasure classes. ◆ The dressage riders, who were all easily 20 years younger than me, and some who were even younger than Tracy, called her the "Indian pony." I didn't mind the good-natured ribbing Tracy and I got on occasion; after all, she was a descendent of Chief Joseph's band of Nez Perce horses, and

Mallory Allen riding Strong Principles. 2006 Appaloosa National Youth Show. Photo by Jennie Wandler.

she was small compared to the Hanoverians and other warmbloods in the barn. ◆
Tracy and I took a lot of ribbing, but for the most part we ignored it. Tracy only cared about being with other horses and in maintaining her rank in the herd, which, it turned out, was still number one. She'd had an excellent teacher in Blackie, and at this new barn, she wasted no time in putting her lessons into practice. What surprised me was that I was apparently the only person who noticed. It was a quiet joy made even more pleasurable by my realization that, while the dressage riders may have known a great deal about riding horses in the arena, they sure didn't know much about getting along with horses when they were on the horses' turf. ◆ Late one drizzly spring evening as I leaned on a fence rail in the gathering darkness, feeling melancholy with missing my farm and my own horses, I noticed four of the dressage riders slogging through the muddy pasture, attempting to catch their uncooperative horses. It was a game the horses were winning, and it was fun to watch as the horses demonstrated their dressage training by wheeling away at the last moment, doing side-passes, and executing other dressage movements. The drenched on-foot riders didn't see the magnificent performance since they were behind the action. They also couldn't see that the leader of 'Simon Says' was Tracy, who cavorted in her own idea of dressage while the other horses gaily followed her. ◆ The drizzle was beginning to soak through my coat as I leaned on the fence rail, and I knew from my own experience over the years how miserable those soaked, horseless riders were out there in the pasture. In another few minutes I took pity on them, and with Tracy's lead rope slung over my shoulder, I walked to the pasture gate and hollered, 'Blackie, dinner!' ◆ Within seconds, Tracy and her pasture pals were at the gate. It took several minutes for the exhausted riders to stumble up to the horses standing quietly behind Tracy. When each rider had clipped her lead rope to her respective horse's halter, I clipped my lead rope onto Tracy's and sedately led her towards the barn. One of the riders asked, 'What method did you use to train Tracy to come so quickly?' ◆ I chuckled, and I could swear Tracy did too. In fact, I was sure I saw Blackie duck around the corner of the barn, whinnying softly in pleasure. 'It's called real-life training,' I replied, hiding my grin. ◆ The next day there was a basket of apples and carrots in front of Tracy's stall and a thank-you note for me. And from that day on, there were no more jokes about the Indian pony.

Photographer Biographies

Jason Abbott

Boise, Idaho

Jason Abbott grew up in the Idaho Palouse countryside and now works and resides with his family and pond fish in Boise, where he enjoys studying and practicing photography. More of Jason's work can be viewed at www.flickr.com/photos/boise.

Jan Bard

Bar-D Ranch

Maple Valley, Washington

www.sirwrangler.com

Jan Bard, along with family Joe, Sydney, Linze, and Lucas, own and operate the Bar-D Ranch in Maple Valley, Washington. Their Hall of Fame Appaloosa stallion, Sir Wrangler, produced over 200 foals at the ranch. Although Jan is a respiratory therapist at Virginia Mason Hospital in Seattle, her passions have been photography and trail riding all her life. To go riding with Jan means the chance to stop on ledges for photos.

Jillian Paige Dunkleberger

Gouverneur, New York

Jillian is a 20-year-old math major studying at SUNY Potsdam in New York and intends to go into teaching once she graduates with her master's. Her photography focuses on her parents' scenic Sawyer Creek Appaloosa farm that is nestled in the heart of the Adirondack region of New York. There, the tradition of breeding quality Appaloosas has been passed down through generations of the Kreider family and is home to World and National Champions.

Jillian's photographs have been featured in *Horse Illustrated* and *Western Side* (Italy). In addition, her photos are used in equine catalogs and ApHC promotional literature, including the award-winning ApHC calendar. More of Jillian's work can be seen at www.sawyercreek.com.

Lisa Estridge

Palisades Appaloosas

Lancaster, Kentucky

www.palisadesapps.com

Lisa's Appaloosa breeding farm is family owned and tended. It sits atop the Palisades of the Kentucky River. The 280 acres where their Appaloosas graze and run are dedicated as conservation land, never to be developed. This area where the Palisades have formed is unique, and the Nature Conservancy is working hard to preserve it.

Palisades' goal is to breed colorful, well-mannered Appaloosas with a variety of backgrounds, including foundation bloodlines as well as more modern additions. Some of the bloodlines you will find include HaDar Shado, Dreamfinder, Goer, Nugget Jim, Prince Plaudit, Mighty Tim, the Sully leopards, and Sundance, to name just a few.

All of Palisades' Appaloosas are handled each day by family, friends, and visitors. Any horses that they find are not suitable for a family farm move on to new homes. Disposition has come first in their Appaloosas, followed by conformation, color, and breeding.

Monika Hannawacker

Schönaúak, Germany

Monika bought her first Appaloosa, Dear Little Cisco, in 1995. She competed in trail and equitation, winning the European champion in open trail and the German champion in non-pro and open trail. In addition, she's trained Cisco to perform circus tricks.

Monika bought a sorrel leopard yearling, Tobys Spot Carlito, in Austria in 2002 and competed in hunter classes with him, and this spring she purchased 2-year-old Ready Dream Dust, a Dreamfinder grandson.

In addition to showing her horses, Monika loves photographing them. Her photos have been published in *Appaloosa Journal*, the Appaloosa Calendar, and other horse publications.

Daria Killinger

Equiscape Photography

Birchrunville, Pennsylvania

www.dlkillingerphoto.com

A practicing equine attorney, Daria has loved animals all her life; dogs, cats, birds, and particularly horses, her menagerie fluctuates, but it's a constant source of entertainment. To counteract the rigors of corporate law (past life), Daria found left-brain expression in her camera, and a ready cast of subjects underfoot. Until recently, she enjoyed the results, and shared them only with close friends and family. Encouragement can be a dangerous thing in the hands of friends—suffice it to say, she entered a few photo contests with modest success. Thus, spurred onward, she now offers her photographic services on a commission basis. "My love and knowledge of horses and animals in general, together with a bit of 'natural' talent (and lots of luck), has enabled me to often capture the essence of the relationship between these amazing creatures and their significant providers."

Ursula Lise

Niebert, The Netherlands

www.invied.com

Ursula has loved animals her entire life. After marrying Wiebe Lise, the couple acquired many animals on their farm. She suffered from leukemia in 2002 and fully recovered after a bone marrow transplant from one of her brothers. After that, Ursula's husband gave her a digital camera, and her love of photography started. She photographs animals daily, but her favorite subject is their 2000 Appaloosa stallion, Invied.

Kevin Pullen

Pullman, Washington

Kevin Pullen was born and raised in northeast Oregon, where he spent much of his time on his grandparents' ranch. There he was able to experience the outdoors and learn an appreciation for hard work and the natural world. As a child, his grandmother would take him on walks down the country road, stopping to peer into wild rose bushes at the young blackbirds in their nests. He continued his interest in nature as a field biologist, presenter, and university zoology instructor.

"I originally delved into photography to better represent the natural world to my students. It suited me nicely as a means of spending time in the outdoors I so enjoy. My work as a naturalist and biologist has provided ample opportunity to photograph. It has produced many interesting experiences as well!

"There is beauty and wonder all around us; capturing it on film is a gratifying challenge. I especially enjoy photographing wildlife. Animals lead rich lives filled with drama and humor. The more time I spend with them, the more their worlds open up to me. The reward of taking photos is that I get to preserve what I observe and share it with others...there is a story behind every photograph.

"I choose to produce unmanipulated images...no electronic alterations have been made to any print. The colors represented are true to the scene."

Jeri Rainer

Rainer's Portrait Studio

Moscow, Idaho

www.rainersportraits.com

Jeri Marie Rainer has been in the portrait industry for 27 years and has worked as a portrait photographer for the last 15 years. She is the recipient of several awards and honors, including recognition as one of the top photographers by the Professional Photographers of Idaho for five years in a row, and three Kodak gallery awards. She and her husband, Paul, live in Moscow, Idaho, and own Rainer's Portrait Studio.

Richard Reed

Aubrey, Texas

www.toskhara.com

Dick and his wife operate the Diamond R Ranch, where they breed Arabian horses and own Appaloosas and Quarter Horses. Dick is an avid equine photographer.

Kristin Reiter

Oak Harbor, Washington

Award-winning writer and photographer Kristen Reiter, DVM, received her first Appaloosa in 1982. Intrigued by their history and fascinated by their colorful coat patterns, she became an instant devotee. Since then, Kristen has participated in countless equine events, with the most notable being the prestigious National Appaloosa Show and the historic Chief Joseph Trail Ride.

Kristen's interest in photography has spanned over 25 years, but her talents flourished when her husband presented her with her first digital camera. She believes that horses and humans possess an extraordinary bond and strives to capture that connection through her candid photographic works.

Diane Rice

Moscow, Idaho

A native of Evanston, Illinois, Diane E. Rice has enjoyed a lifelong love of horses. She returned to school after the birth of her fifth daughter and earned a bachelor's degree in agricultural journalism, with a minor emphasis in animal science, from the University of Wisconsin–Madison in 1997. Upon graduation, she accepted the assistant editor's position at *Appaloosa Journal* and took over the reins as editor in December 2004. She enjoys gardening, home improvement projects, reading, church activities, and spending time with her family.

Sue Schembri

Char-O-Lot Ranch

Myakka City, Florida

www.charolotranch.com

Char-O-Lot Ranch is home to many top breeding Appaloosas and Quarter Horses. Using the most advanced technologies and 30 years of experience in breeding, the staff at Char-O-Lot offers support and advice to mare owners, leaving nothing to chance.

As owners of the famous Appaloosa stallion The Hunter, the Schembris have won the leading breeder award at the World Show four times, having produced and shown hundreds of National and World champions in halter and performance. Sue takes all the photos of their horses.

Brandy Segner

Powell's Imaging and Photography

Marysville, Ohio

www.powellsimaging.com

Kim Utke

Sheldak Ranch

Sheldon, North Dakota

www.sheldakranch.com

Kim Utke is an avid Appaloosa breeder and photographer. She and her husband own Sheldak Ranch, which is dedicated to raising the richest-bred Appaloosas in the industry—priceless pedigrees where every sire and dam in four generations is a champion and/or champion producer. Their bloodlines have known no equal in producing versatile, proven performers with ultimate halter conformation and un-matched dispositions. Sheldak has purchased and bred the very best Lane Hudson, Carl Miles, Cecil Dobbin, and Hank Wiescamp horses for their breeding program. All of them go back to the foundation Appaloosa Old Fred, and they are now infusing the blood of String Of Stars.

Jennie Wandler

Pullman, Washington

Jennie Wandler is a writer/editor and budding photojournalist living in eastern Washington's Palouse area. She has a great passion for horses, especially her Thoroughbred, Sandy, and Hooch, her first horse love, who happened to be an Appaloosa. The only being she adores more than horses is her husband Sam—the love of her life.

Kim Welch

TW Show Horses

www.twshowhorses.com

Kim Welch and her husband, Tom, breed, train, and show Appaloosas. TW Show
Horses is home to many top bloodlines, including Doncha Wanna Moon Me. Tom
and Kim have formed a partnership with other Ohio Appaloosa breeders called the
Ohio Color Connection, which have all pooled their stallion resources together to
offer a wide selection of breeding potential.

Jessica Wright

Boise, Idaho

Jessica Wright grew up in the Pacific Northwest and now lives with her family in
Boise, Idaho, where she continues to pursue an interest in photography that began
with a high school apprenticeship on the Olympic Peninsula.

An American Presence

Haines, Francis. *Appaloosa*. Caballus Publishers, Amon Carter Museum of Art, ApHC. Second edition, 1972, p. 10.

Erskine, Wood. *Life of Charles Erskine Scott Wood*. Rose Wind Press, Vancouver, WA, 1991, p. 22.

Linker, Ray. "Gift horse fulfils 105-year-old promise." *The Observer.* July 28, 1997, p. 22.

Babies, Babies

Lose, M. Phyllis. *Blessed Are the Broodmares*. Copyright 1978, 1991 by M. Phyllis Lose, V.M.D. Reprinted with permission of John Wiley & Sons, Inc., p.85.

At Work and Play

Taylor, Henry. *The Flying Change*. Louisiana State University Press, Baton Rouge, 1985, p. 50, p. 151.

About the Author

Cheryl Dudley is a freelance writer for various publications, including the *Appaloosa Journal*. She is also a full-time writer for the University of Idaho, and holds a master's degree in English from there. She lives in Moscow, Idaho, with her husband, Don, and their four horses.

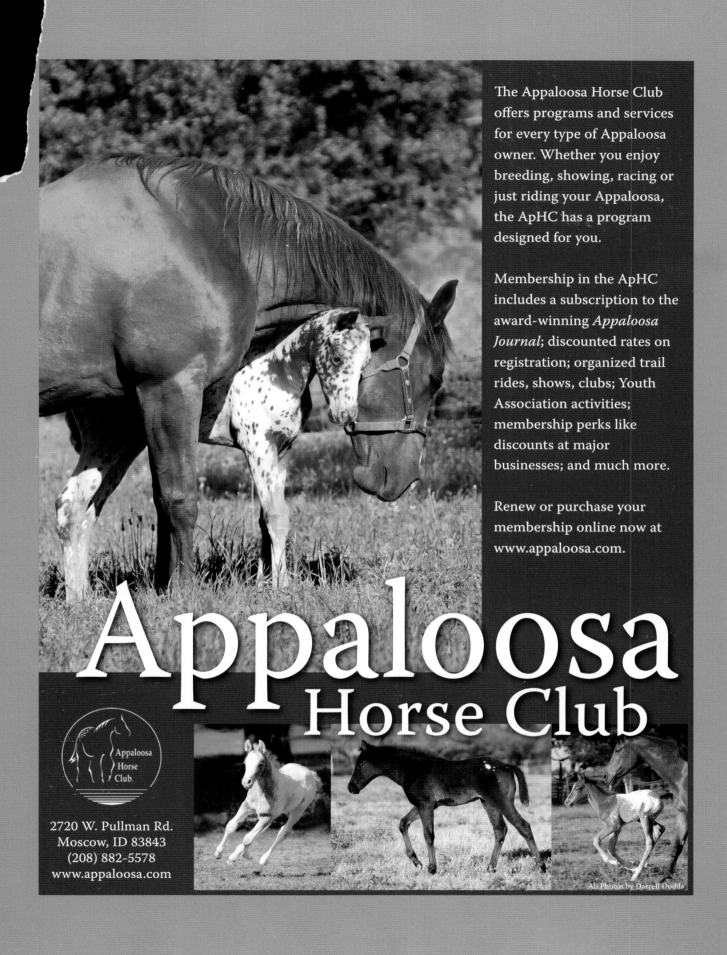